A TROLLOPE CHRONOLOGY

Macmillan Author Chronologies

General Editor: Norman Page, Professor of Modern English
Literature, University of Nottingham

Reginald Berry
A POPE CHRONOLOGY

Edward Bishop
A VIRGINIA WOOLF CHRONOLOGY

Timothy Hands
A GEORGE ELIOT CHRONOLOGY

Norman Page
A BYRON CHRONOLOGY
A DICKENS CHRONOLOGY

F. B. Pinion
A WORDSWORTH CHRONOLOGY

R. C. Terry
A TROLLOPE CHRONOLOGY

Further titles in preparation

THE GOOD ST. ANTHONY

KEPT HIS EYES FIRMLY FIXED UPON HIS BOOK.

THE WAY THAT VERY PAST WRITER, MR. TROLLOPE, COLLECTED THE INFORMATION THAT ENABLED HIM TO BRAND OUR GIRLS AS GONERILS AND REGANS.

'The Good St Anthony' from Melbourne *Punch*, 17 April 1873 (by courtesy of the State Library of Victoria, Melbourne, Australia).

A Trollope Chronology

R. C. TERRY

Professor of English
University of Victoria, British Columbia

MACMILLAN
PRESS

First published 1989

Published by
THE MACMILLAN PRESS LTD
Houndmills, Basingstoke, Hampshire RG21 2XS
and London
Companies and representatives
throughout the world

Typeset by Wessex Typesetters
(Division of The Eastern Press Ltd)
Frome, Somerset

Printed in Hong Kong

British Library Cataloguing in Publication Data
Terry, R. C.
A Trollope chronology.—(Macmillan author
chronologies).
1. Trollope, Anthony—Biography
2. Novelists, English—19th century—
Biography
I. Title
823'.8   PR5686
ISBN 0–333–39914–5

For Leslie and Laura

'I listen, but am silent'
(motto of Sir John Trollope and family)

Contents

Contents

General Editor's Preface

Most biographies are ill adapted to serve as works of reference –
not surprisingly so, since the biographer is likely to regard his
function as the devising of a continuous and readable narrative,
with excursions into interpretation and speculation, rather than a
bald recital of facts. There are times, however, when anyone
reading for business or pleasure needs to check a point quickly or
to obtain a rapid overview of part of an author's life or career; and
at such moments turning over the pages of a biography can be a
time-consuming and frustrating occupation. The present series of
volumes aims at providing a means whereby the chronological
facts of an author's life and career, rather than needing to be prised
out of the narrative in which they are (if they appear at all) securely
embedded, can be seen at a glance. Moreover, whereas biographies
are often, and quite understandably, vague over matters of fact
(since it makes for tediousness to be forever enumerating details
of dates and places), a chronology can be precise whenever it is
possible to be precise.

Thanks to the survival, sometimes in very large quantities, of
letters, diaries, notebooks and other documents, as well as to
thoroughly researched biographies and bibliographies, this material
now exists in abundance for many major authors. In the case of,
for example, Dickens, we can often ascertain what he was doing in
each month and week, and almost on each day, of his prodigiously
active working life; and the student of, say, *David Copperfield* is
likely to find it fascinating as well as useful to know just when
Dickens was at work on each part of that novel, what other literary
enterprises he was engaged in at the same time, whom he was
meeting, what places he was visiting, and what were the relevant
circumstances of his personal and professional life. Such a chronology is not, of course, a substitute for a biography; but its
arrangement, in combination with its index, makes it a much more
convenient tool for this kind of purpose; and it may be acceptable
as a form of 'alternative' biography, with its own distinctive
advantages as well as its obvious limitations.

Since information relating to an author's early years is usually
scanty and chronologically imprecise, the opening section of some
volumes in this series groups together the years of childhood and

adolescence. Thereafter each year, and usually each month, is dealt with separately. Information not readily assignable to a specific month or day is given as a general note under the relevant year or month. The first entry for each month carries an indication of the day of the week, so that when necessary this can be readily calculated for other dates. Each volume also contains a bibliography of the principal sources of information. In the chronology itself, the sources of many of the more specific items, including quotations, are identified, in order that the reader who wishes to do so may consult the original contexts.

NORMAN PAGE

Introduction

That distinguished Trollopian Bradford Booth once referred to Anthony Trollope as the busiest man of Victorian letters.[1] Commentators have always marvelled at the phenomenal energy – let alone organising ability – which enabled Trollope to pursue two careers simultaneously, first as servant of the Post Office for over 33 years, and second as highly successful man of letters, eventually producing 47 novels, five volumes of short stories, four substantial travel books, and other non-fiction, including biographical sketches of Lord Palmerston and Thackeray, studies of Caesar's *Commentaries* and a *Life of Cicero*, plus a vast amount of periodical journalism as yet not entirely accounted for. In addition he maintained a full round of social and business engagements, rode with manic ferocity to hounds all season, made almost daily visits to his clubs – he had membership of three at least – and led a satisfying home life, reading, relaxing and entertaining professional colleagues and friends. He also made extensive journeys, thereby surely earning him the right to be called most travelled man of Victorian letters as well as the busiest.

Particularly in his case, then, a chronology needs no justification. It provides a vivid insight into a peculiarly driven individual, impelled from his earliest years to escape from poverty and isolation, and, triumphing as a man, to become the epitome of the Victorian work ethic and belief in self-help. Trollope was a man who could not keep still. Thus the daily records, presented in the abbreviated form of this series, make an intensely dramatic study which, it is hoped, will increase the reader's understanding of the man and enjoyment of his work. Trollope's hyperactive nature and appetite for work were well known to his contemporaries – a matter of envy, admiration and amusement. Few of his circle were unaware of his machine-like productivity, so often condemned by reviewers, and he boasted openly of starting a new novel as soon as its predecessor was laid aside. His praise of Sir Walter Scott living at '20 horse power of vivacity' (*L*, II, 660) might well have applied to himself, and he took pride in living 'at a perpetual gallop' (*L*, I, 30) to the end of his life, when, troubled by angina and asthma, he would still leap from a railway carriage before the train had come to a stop (*I & R*, p. 232).[2] He was good for 16 hours a day, said his friend Cuthbert Bede, who proved the point when they were together at a country-house weekend party. Up at the crack of dawn – Trollope had a five-o'clock-in-the-morning genius – he fell at once to his writing, completing his quota before breakfast time. He could then, he said, take his pleasure (in this case hunting and cards) with a clear conscience. Bede explains,

> When I left the house after dinner it was nearly eleven o'clock and Mr Trollope was then playing whist. I had promised to rejoin them at breakfast at half-past nine; and I found Mr Trollope already downstairs and busied with the morning's postal delivery. He was in hunting costume, and I complimented him on his freshness and industry, after his late hours of the preceding night, when he cheerily replied that he had never felt better in his life, and that he had got up at five o'clock. 'Since then,' he said, 'I have earned twenty pounds by my pen; besides writing several needful letters.'   (*I & R*, p. 108)[3]

At home his routine seldom altered: the early-morning call, coffee and three hours at the desk before he proceeded to the Post Office at St Martin's le Grand; an afternoon call at the club for a rubber of whist; and most evenings engagements of one kind or another. Anne Thackeray, visiting at Waltham House, corroborates, adding the delicious touch to her recollection that if the novelist did *not* get up when called he gave his man half-a-crown: ' "The labourer is worthy of his hire!" said Mr Trollope in his deep cheerful lispy voice' (*I & R*, p. 88).[4] Trollope, we know, could get by with little sleep; he was one of those lucky mortals with the Churchillian knack of taking forty winks at will. For all that, he had what his friend T. H. S. Escott called an iron constitution,[5] the endowment of genes from his mother, the indomitable Frances Trollope, who set to, at the age of 50, to write novels and save her large family from ruin, while Anthony's ailing father, failed lawyer and amateur farmer, Thomas Anthony, slowly disintegrated in morose silence broken by half-crazed outbursts of anger. The inheritance of good health, as capricious as literary inspiration, scarcely lighted upon the rest of the family: of the children, Henry, Arthur, Emily, Cecilia (another Emily expired the day of her birth) all died young; Thomas Adolphus, Anthony's elder brother *did* achieve literary success, but nothing like his brother's. Given to indolence himself, he wrote in some wonderment of Anthony's appetite for work: 'Work to him was a necessity and a satisfaction' (*WIR*, I, 358–9). And indeed it was – the highest human felicity, Anthony was to say on many occasions, whether slogging away at his desk in the Post Office, eyes bulging and a handkerchief stuffed in his mouth, or writing a novel in the bowels of some pitching ocean liner. He drove his pen, Henry James observed, 'as steadily on the tumbling ocean as in Montagu Square [his London home between 1873 and 1880]'. If that was not genius, James implied, it was the nearest thing to it (*I & R*, p. 201).[6] Trollope, of course, strenuously debunked genius and inspiration, crediting himself only with pertinacity, strength of purpose and sheer love of the trade. He was, in our terms, a workaholic. What he most dreaded from old age was immobility, and his hope of an after-life was contingent upon the 'disembodied and beatified spirits' still wanting novels in paradise (*L*, II, 548).

Such a colourful and busy figure is therefore admirably suited for the Author Chronologies series, and its limited focus on dates and events connected by brief linking commentary throws dramatic light on the increasing momentum of Trollope's activities over a period of some 60 years. Notes and explanatory matter are kept to the minimum and introduced in square brackets in the text to give continuity and maintain an appropriate pace of narrative. The Chronology begins with Trollope's parents and family as a context for the trials of his childhood (well known to readers of the *Autobiography*). Items concerning his early background, where information is sparse, show something of the love and loyalty within the family circle to counteract the dominant strain of Anthony's account of a childhood and adolescence marked by utter wretchedness, self-loathing and isolation. Trollope's early years in the Post Office, the next section of this volume, promised little but a repetition of his dismal schooldays: shoddy, ill-tempered and slack at his desk, he mooned through his working day and wasted his free time. As he says in the *Autobiography*, 'I must certainly acknowledge that the first seven years of my official life were neither creditable to myself nor useful to the public service' (p. 37).

A feature of this period brought to light by the recent research of Helen Heineman is the importance of family ties and particularly his mother's concern for the junior clerk in the Post Office. It was her connection with Sir Francis Freeling, Secretary to the Post Office, that gave him his start in November 1834, and for the next seven years (despite his emphasis on the isolation of his London existence) Frances Trollope exercised a deep concern over his health and happiness, as well as trying to further his literary ambitions.[7] In this respect it is also interesting to note Anthony's own desire to find creative outlets both in writing and keeping track of his reading by means of a diary. But in his everyday job he floundered from one scrape to another; again modern research has filled in some gaps. As R. H. Super has observed, the evidence of minute-books from Post Office sources shows him a most unpromising public servant. Lt-Col. William Maberly, who had succeeded Freeling, noted in 1839 that Trollope was bringing discredit to his department 'by the want of proper attention to his duty'.[8] By nature rebellious and stubborn, Trollope seems to have gone out of his way to antagonise his superiors, first Maberly, and then Sir Rowland Hill, with whom (he later gloated) he had enjoyed 'such delicious feuds' (*Auto.*, p. 244).

Only on his transfer to Ireland, where he moved in September 1841, did he mend his ways. As surveyor's clerk in the Central District he soon became, in his brother's words, 'one of the most efficient and valuable officers in the Post Office (*WIR*, I, 257). We can only surmise the reasons for this miraculous transformation: the chance to make a fresh start, the excitement of the wild, misty Irish landscape after the drab environs of his lodgings in Northumberland Street by the Marylebone workhouse, better health (after a mysterious illness), the salve to his ego of having men under him, the discovery that his naturally aggressive manner went down well with the wild and rowdy Irish. Moving into society he came into contact, through Sir William Gregory of Coole Park, Dublin, with writers and artists. In the resort of Kingstown in July 1842, he met Rose Heseltine and fell in love. They married in June 1844, and had two sons, Henry Merivale (b. 1846) and Frederic James Anthony (b. 1847). Anthony turned to writing and, with greater enthusiasm than ever, to his Civil Service career, bullying subordinates, riding down upon hapless managers of rural sub-post offices, devising more efficient mail routes and at one time catching a defaulting manageress who had been opening the mails and pocketing any cash. This resulted in a court case in which Anthony stood against the powerful attorney, and later leader of the Home Rule party, Isaac Butt and won.[9]

The problem for a chronology in dealing with a daily ritual of journeys on behalf of the Post Office is sheer volume, and, to avoid a catalogue of tedious repetition, editorial policy has been to summarise the itinerary, a practice similarly followed with respect to his postal duties and travels elsewhere. The reader can imagine the zeal and capability of the young official whose ambition was, he later declared (once his territory had widened to southern England) 'to cover the country with rural letter-carriers' (*Auto.*, p. 77). As in Ireland, his coverage of England, Wales and Scotland during the 1850s is best conveyed in a work such as this by brief survey, rather than lengthy account. For the zealous public servant kept records of his daily journeys, meticulously, though often illegibly, in six notebooks; it was important to keep such accounts, since part of his income depended on expenses to augment his regular stipend (beginning at £100 a year in the Central District of Ireland). These records (now in the Morris L. Parrish Collection of the Library of Princeton University) show more eloquently than anything I have read the energy and industry of the young officer.

Between 1841 and the end of 1857, the year which marks a break with his mostly Irish sojourn (after travel to the West Indies and various duties in England he became permanently settled as Surveyor of the Eastern District of England in November 1859), the list of places he visited from various bases at various times – Banagher, Kingstown, Drumsna, Clonmel and Cork – runs into hundreds. To dwell on his daily itinerary is out of the question, but some illustrations from the mass of material can be given as a measure of his industry. Between 15 September and 5 December 1841, he apparently covered some 546 Irish miles (translated as 685.4 English miles). Mostly he rode, but sometimes he took a coach. In the month of November he notched 40 miles some days, even touching 65 on two occasions. He got back to Banagher for Christmas Day dinner (perhaps covering 32 miles to do so) and had a four-day break. The following year he managed things better, getting back to Banagher on the 23rd for five days' holiday. Drumsna is prominent in 1843, especially in the month of September, when, as the *Autobiography* explains, walking with his friend, John Merivale, he stumbled across a ruined house which provided the opening scene for his first novel, *The Macdermots of Ballycloran* (1847). After Sunday 9 June there is a largely blank page in the first book and across it one word 'married'. The wedding took place on 11 June 1844. Names of more southerly places figure in the years 1844–50, with Cork, Killarney and Mallow prominent, for he had been transferred to the Southern District at the end of August 1844.

By mid-1851 his itineraries show a succession of west-of-England destinations: Bristol (1 Aug), Exeter (2–3 Aug), Plymouth (4 Aug); then he is on to Sidmouth and other towns and villages in Devon. Scenic description is somewhat rare in Trollope's novels, but treasured memories of the Devon lanes occur in *Rachel Ray* (1863):

> It was now in July, when the summer sun is at the hottest, – and in those southern parts of Devonshire the summer sun in July is very hot. There is no other part of England like it. The lanes are low and narrow, and not a breath of air stirs through them. The ground rises in hills on all sides, so that every spot is a sheltered nook. The rich red earth drinks in the heat and holds it, and no breezes come up from the southern torpid sea. Of all counties in England Devonshire is the fairest to the eye; but, having known it in its summer glory, I must confess that those southern regions are not fitted for much noonday summer walking.   (Ch. 2)

And Trollope in the 1850s had much summer walking in the noonday sun, visiting sub-post offices and barking a stream of questions at their often bemused managers. At Budleigh Salterton, probably in June 1852, he called on the rector, a fellow Wykehamist, whose son, T. H. S. Escott, was to become his first biographer. The notation after 5 August 1852 is 'Deduct cost of sending family to S. Wales' (£2 11s. according to his expenses). In this period also he crossed to Jersey and Guernsey, where, on his urging, the first trial of pillar letter boxes was made. In parts of Cornwall he continued revising rural posts; a witness from those days recalls him stalking into one office 'booted and spurred, much to the consternation of the maiden lady in charge'. One messenger was so flustered that he clapped into his hat a number of penny stamps, which stuck to his head in the heat. 'Mr Trollope roared at the fun, and brought the man back, stamps and all, so that the aid of a barber might be invoked to release him from his predicament' (*I & R*, pp. 45–6). More sifting of these fascinating diaries will increase awareness of Trollope's vigour in public service.

Gradual, if slow, promotion eventually put Trollope into the international sphere of survey, diplomatic negotiation and travel, beginning with a mission to the Middle East, where his task was to secure advantageous mail routes from the Nubar Bey. It was typical of his thoroughness that he tested the speed of laden camels. On another important assignment, to the West Indies, he prepared himself on the voyage by 'talking to the officers of his ship about such technical matters as the effect of prevailing winds on the speed of vessels of different sizes, the condition of navigable passages between islands, and the location of suitable alternate harbours'.[10] His recommendations delighted his superiors at St Martin's le Grand. Nowhere are his powers of working hard while constantly on the move more evident, however, than in the chronology of his first visit to North America, in 1861–2, during which he visited over 30 towns and cities in Canada and the United States. On his second trip to the United States (1868) he suffered the heated cauldron of Washington in June, and the importunate manners of some of his hosts. One in particular, an American senator, proposed dining with him every day while he was in Washington. But there were many more agreeable friends to look up, notably Kate Field, whom he adored, and the literati of Boston.[11] Once again, the reader must divine behind the roster of names and dates and places the demands upon Trollope's nerve and constitution. The analogy comes to mind of the twentieth-century reading tour in which the celebrity is paraded from bookshop to campus to Rotary Club luncheon in one constant performance, which at the end produces catatonic trance and total exhaustion. Put Trollope's itineraries over a century ago in this context with the conditions of long-distance travel, and one can readily appreciate his phenomenal energy.

When Trollope retired from the Post Office in October 1867 his farewell dinner in London was attended by nearly 100 people. The usual facetious merriment of such occasions was doubtless observed, but the parting after almost 33 years was keenly felt, as passages in the *Autobiography* suggest. 'And so the cord was cut,' he writes, 'and I was a free man to run about the world where I would' (p. 245). Trollope's running about the world is one theme of this chronology, which follows in some detail some of his most exciting journeys, to Australia and New Zealand twice (1871–2 and 1875) and South Africa (1877). Again, from the bare facts of itineraries the reader can gauge something of the spirit and resourcefulness of the tireless traveller Booth called him. Unlike earlier expeditions to the West Indies and America, these, undertaken by a man getting past his prime, posed special hardships. In New Zealand he and Rose made a hazardous journey from Lawrence to Milton through one of the worst snowstorms of the winter. When their coach was blocked by huge snowdrifts, in typical fashion Anthony helped their driver clear a way, confessing that he was 'more at ease with a pen than a shovel'. Rose Trollope, no less mettlesome, negotiated part of the road on foot, her petticoats balled up with snow making her 'an enormous size, and a wonderful sight to behold' (*I & R*, p. 184). Once home, she gave pithy accounts of their journeys to the Blackwoods. Trollope's second visit to Australia and the trip to South Africa, made without Rose, proved even more arduous. Although the old stamina is there, his letters ring with homesickness. Trollope wrote from Port Elizabeth in August 1877, 'I own I look forward with dread to some of the journeys I shall have to make on post cars. Five hundred miles at a stretch, – with four five or six hours allowed at night according to the fancies of the black drivers' (*L*, II, 734). From these journeys, with the added strains of public appearances and receptions, emerged the usual quota of fiction and travel books.

Other kinds of travels emerge significantly in the Chronology. These have not been given much attention to date, but they seem to me typical of the rhythms of Trollope's life. Regular vacations were an essential characteristic of a writer renowned for his consistency and continuity. From the earliest days in Ireland he used periods of leave from the Post Office for holidays; indeed, combining pleasure with business, he courted Rose at the seaside resort where her banker father had brought the family from smoky Rotherham. Florence, where his brother Tom acquired the Villino Trollope, a centre thereafter for expatriate English artists, was a regular haunt over the years. Here, in the early 1860s, Kate Field had the opportunity of observing the two brothers, remarking 'the almost boyish enthusiasm and impulsive argumentation' of Anthony, alongside Tom – 'half Socrates and half Galileo' (*I & R*, p. 72). As Trollope's career progressed, more ambitious trips were planned, mostly to France, Holland, Germany and Switzerland, the resort of Felsenegg, near Zug, being a favourite. This was change of place not pace, for Trollope, like his brother, was a vigorous walker, and, of course, his writing quotas had to be maintained. Once he wrote to George Eliot from Felsenegg, 'Here we are on the top of a mountain, where I write for four hours a day, walk for four hours, eat for two, and sleep out the balance satisfactorily' (*L*, II, 785). Keeping on the move seems to have been part of the Trollope enginery for creation, a necessity of his restless spirit. At the end of his life, research for a novel on agrarian guerrilla warfare took him twice to Ireland, but even then he found time to 'holiday'.

Although the business of a chronology is to catalogue major events in a writer's life, it is important to balance the record with minor happenings, local, domestic, the trivial details which are part of every man's existence. Thus items show the novelist in ordinary circumstances, ordering his cigars, going to the theatre, fooling around on a golf course, swimming in a Scottish lake, complaining about the cost of tobacco, or getting over a sore throat. Insignificant in themselves, they help to give a rounded picture of this warm-hearted, gregarious man. Nothing more effectively among these personal glimpses reveals the man than what we learn through the Chronology of his home life, his generous hospitality and his wide circle of friends, among them the Revd W. Lucas Collins, who recalled evenings at Waltham House where the author, 'very happy . . . amongst his cows, and roses, and strawberries . . . delighted to welcome at his quiet dinner-table some half-dozen of intimate friends'. In the garden on warm summer's evenings, 'wines and fruit were laid out under the fine old cedar tree and many a good story was told while the tobacco-smoke went curling up into the soft twilight'.[12] Here, off duty and out of the limelight, is a very different Trollope from the roaring John Bull of so many contemporary memories. The good fellowship of friends is matched in Trollope's life story by his close family ties. Many items in this record show his concern for his sons' welfare; others refer to his nieces, Beatrice ('Bice') Trollope (Tom's talented daughter) and Florence Bland, who came to live at Waltham in 1863 and was to take dictation of several books as Anthony became increasingly afflicted by writer's cramp.

But at the heart of all this domesticity is Rose Trollope, whose role in the Chronology, though small in reference, is in fact crucial. Rose still remains a figure about whom we know very little, yet she is central to the novelist's existence. She was not, on the face of it, a striking or forceful personality, although the one photograph we have shows a determined line to the jaw and a direct glance. That she was unremarkable on first acquaintance is borne out by several witnesses, among them George Henry Lewes, who noted in his journal for 15 April 1861, 'Went down to Waltham to dine and sleep at Trollope's. He has a charming house and grounds, and I like him very much, so wholesome and straightforward a man. Mrs Trollope did not make any decided impression on me,

one way or another' (*I & R*, p. 136). This is hardly surprising:
marriage to any celebrity can easily endow the partner with a
certain insubstantiality. And, given the conventions of Victorian
marriage and Trollope's own person, it is, on reflection, rather
remarkable that we can see anything of Rose at all. But from
numerous small references and comments of her own we can
assume that she was certainly not a mouse, while Trollope's
fictional presentations of the married state suggest, though not a
Mrs Proudie, a woman of spirit and independence. His guarded
comment in the *Autobiography* about his marriage acknowledges
that she read almost everything he wrote 'to my very great
advantage in matters of taste' (p. 63). Evidently she possessed both
charm and grace. In the early years of their marriage we have
glimpses of tact with her sharp-tongued mother-in-law. Writing
from Mallow in 1848, Frances Trollope notes 'Anthony and his
excellent little wife are as happy as possible'. Rose worked hard
organising outings and picnics; mother-in-law reciprocated, making
early-morning tea; she was not long, said her biographer, 'in
recognizing the excellent influence of the young wife on her son's
life in every way' (*I & R*, p. 19). This is very true. Rose seems to
have dedicated herself to sustaining and promoting Anthony's
career, her chief task over the 29 years of their marriage being to
maintain the domestic order that his high-horsepower career
demanded. Thus, when she left New York for home ahead of him
in 1861, it was, he wrote to Kate Field, because of 'all the stern
necessities of an English home' (*L*, I, 161). Kate was the recipient
of the one instance I have found that shows Rose sometimes had
sarcastic wit. A mutual friend, Isa Blagden, who had been
something of a trial to the Trollope brothers over her publishers,
had just had her second novel published. Rose commented, 'I
hope it will have more common-sense than the former one – it
can't well have less' (*I & R*, p. 139). Scattered references show she
had a lively-enough personality. She kept up with the fashion,
although one observer noticed that at Lord Houghton's reception
at Fryston in 1866 she appeared hatless but with a rose in her
white hair; this was going too far (*I & R*, p. 89). Sir Henry
Brackenbury, a guest at Waltham in 1868, was most impressed by
her beautiful feet. The fastidious Augustus Hare, meeting her in
1877, found her 'a beautiful old lady with snow-white hair turned
back' (*I & R*, p. 151). Rose lived well into her nineties, reticent to
the last about her husband's person and achievement but keeping

in a small red-leather portfolio a treasured memento – 30 letters from eminent men praising his work. Of the couple's mutual affection there can be no doubt. As I have noted elsewhere, this was sometimes shown by Anthony in a clumsy, lumbering humour, as in the inscription he wrote in her copy of his lecture 'On English Prose Fiction', which says, 'Rose Trollope from her obedient slave / The Lecturer'.[13]

There can be no doubt that Rose was endlessly supportive and a supremely efficient organiser of the home. The bond between them remained strong to the end. Julian Hawthorne was probably correct when he wrote that 'his wife was his books, though not at all literary' (*I & R*, p. 147). Anthony's devotion to her is plain to see, especially in the letters of his last years; the degree of his reliance upon her will never be known. For all such human dimensions that go beyond the documentary record of dates and engagements this volume is primarily concerned with, I have drawn upon the *Autobiography*, the *Letters* and my own edition of over a hundred memories by his contemporaries, *Trollope: Interviews and Recollections* (1987). In this way, it is hoped, the Chronology may also serve as partial biographical sketch as well as a great novelist's calendar.

Returning to this book's larger scope, I shall concentrate now on his literary and public role as the most popular personality of the mid-Victorian scene after Dickens. Some idea has already been suggested of the extraordinary powers of concentration and rapid productivity the man showed in his Post Office work. In a letter to an unknown correspondent Trollope wrote, 'Pray know that when a man begins writing a book he never gives over. The evil with which he is beset is as inveterate as drinking – as exciting as gambling' (*L*, i, 43). Or, as Rose jokingly put it, 'He never leaves off . . . and he always has two packages of manuscript in his desk, besides the one he's working on, and the one that's being published' (*I & R*, p. 147). Method and industry was the trick of it, but Trollope also had a turn for speed; stories abound of his contempt for waiting for inspiration and going to work on a novel like a cobbler making a pair of shoes, grinding out 250 words every quarter of an hour for three hours. He could drop his pen almost in mid-sentence, it was said, and resume next morning; and on more than one occasion within days of finishing one book embarked upon another. All this is well documented and can be read in Sadleir and others. What he was more reticent about, however,

and even a little foxy, was the time spent working as the novel
took shape in his mind. From time to time, though, he gives a clue
to the obsessive and demanding nature of the writer's trade, as in
the letter quoted above, or in this eloquent note about characters
in a novel:

> he can never know them well unless he can live with them in
> the full reality of established intimacy. They must be with him
> as he lies down to sleep, and as he wakes from his dreams.
>
> (*Auto.*, p. 200)

Allied with constancy, Trollope had a microwave-oven mind or,
as he put it, a 'capacity for quick roasting'. When Thackeray needed
a novel in a hurry to launch the *Cornhill Magazine* in the spring of
1860, Trollope came to the rescue with *Framley Parsonage*. Over-
production, lack of revision and little time for second thoughts, it
is well known, were the adverse side of Trollope's production line,
but there is no denying his power of rapid composition.

However, it took a long time for Trollope to get started on the
road to literary fame. The Chronology charts this slow process
(after a series of failures), beginning with the reception of *The
Warden* (1855) and *Barchester Towers* (1857); a critical point is reached
by his having a portable tablet made at this time providing him
the means of writing on the move. From now on his career rapidly
advanced. The year 1859 has long been recognised as a landmark
in Trollope's writing, just as by virtue of his West Indies tour it
marks his success in the Civil Service. Something of his official
confidence at this time is manifest in the role he played in
establishing a Post Office Library and Literary Association at St
Martin's le Grand (a little-known venture described in Appendix
B). His literary growth is by far the most dramatic element in the
Chronology at this point, however, and it is indicated by the tone
of reviews. *Dr Thorne* (1858) was greeted as 'one of the extremely
select few who shine out like a constellation among the unnum-
bered lesser luminaries of the "circulating" firmament' (*Leader*, 29
May 1858, pp. 519–20). A general review of some 8000 words,
possibly by R. H. Hutton, appeared in the *National Review* in
October, and next E. S. Dallas, in *The Times* of 23 May 1859,
acknowledged Trollope's eminence among the Mudie readership.
As the *London Review* put it when *Framley Parsonage* came out in

book form, 'Mr Trollope has now got his foot fairly in the stirrup' (II [11 May 1861] 544–5).

The literary record also illustrates added responsibilities such as Trollope's interest in the founding and management of the *Fortnightly Review* from 1865, his contributions to the *Pall Mall Gazette*, and his troubled years as editor of *St Paul's Magazine* from January 1867 until he surrendered the position in either June or July 1870. He was an uncomfortable, though scrupulously diligent, editor and confesses that part of his trouble was his own soft heart. He just could not bring himself to say to a young lady, and, especially to someone he knew, 'My dear friend, my dear friend, this is trash!' (*Auto.*, p. 248). This is only part of the story. Trollope chafed under the bit of journalistic limitations occasioned by the policies of management committees, or of writing to order; when it came to writing he always needed space for his own Pegasus.[14] His best journalistic efforts were those he alone generated, such as his travel letters from Australia (1875) and from South Africa (1877–8), or his eleven articles on 'London tradesmen' for the *Pall Mall Gazette* (1880).

Some of his other literary engagements were more to his taste – for example, membership of the Royal Literary Fund, to which he was enlisted in May 1861, as a steward for the annual dinner. As the Chronology indicates, he became a very active member, serving on the General Committee after March 1864 until the end of his life, and specialising in its financial affairs (he was made Treasurer in March 1869), as well as conscientiously investigating cases of grants and applications for aid. He was often concerned with planning the annual dinner, and gave, or responded to, one of the many toasts which elongated such occasions. At least seven of his speeches are on record. After his death, the General Committee of the Fund passed an elaborate resolution of gratitude which was forwarded to Rose with a letter from Lord John Manners attesting 'to the anxiety he constantly manifested that the relief administered . . . should be efficacious and generous'. For Rose, another cherished souvenir.[15]

Trollope's service in the public sphere was by no means limited to the Post Office and the Royal Literary Fund. He was keenly interested in what went on around him and, being a celebrity with access to other men of mark, was often called upon for donations and public appearances. Several of the worthy causes he took up and the lectures he gave in support of them are to be found in the calendar of events of his later years. His second journey to the United States on Post Office affairs (1868) also found him looking into the longstanding aggravation concerning an international law of copyright. His understanding of this question caused him to be invited to sit on the Royal Commission on Copyright in 1873, and, once again, his energetic contributions proved timely and helpful.

His social, political and particularly educational concerns became increasingly part of his routine, with lectures up and down the country. These are worthy of far more scrutiny than a chronology allows and raise interesting issues about a hitherto unexplored aspect of my subject. What topics did Trollope choose to speak in public about? When and where? How effective was he on the platform? In the final section of this Introduction brief consideration will be given to these questions. A tentative checklist of his major speeches is provided in Appendix A.

Among his best-known lectures, 'The Civil Service as a Profession' (1861) was construed by some senior colleagues, Rowland Hill in particular, as lobbying against promotion by merit and an inflammatory case for extending the privileges of civil servants. 'On English Prose Fiction as a Rational Amusement' (1864) sought to vindicate his profession against contemporary criticism on the familiar score of morals and time-wasting. 'The Present Condition of the Northern States of the American Union' (1863) arose from his interest in American affairs and the effect of the Civil War. 'The Higher Education of Women' (privately printed, 1868), his fourth major address, was printed soon after he took up duties as editor of *St Paul's Magazine* in autumn 1867.[16] Other lectures included 'Politics as a Daily Study for Common People' (1864), 'The Native Races of South Africa' (or 'The Condition of Zulu People') (1878), 'The National Gallery' (1861), which he wrote but did not present, and 'The Best Means of Extending and Securing an International Law of Copyright' (1866), which was read at the congress of the National Association for the Promotion of Social Science in Manchester in October 1866.

Speeches incorporating the above materials and themes were a regular part of his public life. One such, 'The Art of Reading', was delivered at the second annual prize-giving of the Quebec Institute in 1876 and repeated at a prize-giving in the City and Spitalfields School of Art. W. P. Frith, the artist, and a close friend, was also speaking on the latter occasion, and noted afterwards, 'Trollope made a good speech, and I made a bad one.'[17] This grace note need not be taken too seriously. Although, as a trained civil servant, Trollope could marshal his arguments and deliver them forcibly, he was no better surely than Thackeray and miles behind Dickens as a public speaker. Self-conscious to a degree on the podium, he would have displayed himself by rather elaborate oratory, and the language of his speeches I have read indicates somewhat stilted, sententious utterance, though not without flashes of humour. He was not a natural performer, as Dickens was, and waxing eloquent he became over-excited. Once, at a conference on the Eastern Question in St James's Hall (Dec 1876), Thomas Hardy noted that Trollope over-ran the time limit, and the chairman, having desperately rung a bell which Trollope ignored, finally tugged at his coat-tails, only to have Trollope exclaim parenthetically, 'Please leave my coat alone', and continue to hold forth (*I & R*, p. 219). Details of his electioneering speeches as candidate for Beverley in the General Election of 1867 are sparse, but reveal a capacity to think on his feet and handle barracking. Rather more is now known of his speeches at the Royal Literary Fund annual dinners, but again the impression is of the amateur actor 'on stage' and therefore rather grandiose.

One suspects that in an age of public lecturing Trollope knew his limitations. He certainly regarded the preparation and time involved as a chore and, unlike Dickens and Thackeray, saw in the new fad no source of additional income. In fact on one occasion at least he was critical of Dickens for his capacity to make money at it. He wrote, 'To me the labour of preparing a lecture is considerable' (he was asking a small fee of £20), enlarging on the task in another letter to the same correspondent,

> I have no aptitude or taste for lecturing on subjects other than such as may crop up and interest me at the moment. To prepare a lecture is to me a work of labour, occupying me a fortnight. It is an employment which is neither lucrative, nor except at the time of delivery, pleasant. (*L*, II, 833)

Yet Trollope was generous with his services. When the Secretary of Glasgow Athenaeum, Henry Johnston, rather timidly inquired whether he would come and talk to members, Trollope brushed aside all question of a fee: ' "Do not speak of terms", he said; "when a man has something to say, and a suitable place and opportunity are offered to him for saying it, that should be sufficient for him." ' He would not even ask for travel expenses and concluded, 'I'll come . . . but say no more about money' (*I & R*, p. 216).

By and large Trollope's public utterances went down well. The political statement on the Bulgarian atrocities referred to above was sufficiently John Bullish to elicit warm applause and cheers, especially when, according to the *Pall Mall Gazette*, he spoke of the Turk as 'incurable', incapable of judging between good and evil, and capable of all manner of tyranny, cruelty and oppression. 'He was the worst citizen in the world' and would have to be made to live in Europe under totally different laws and customs. At this there were loud cries of 'Hear, hear' (*I & R*, p. 170).

Trollope spoke trenchantly on American affairs, sticking by his advocacy of the North in the Civil War according to his travel book, *North America* published in May 1862 (popular English opinion sided with the South) and delighting his audiences with tongue-in-cheek sarcasms about Americans. At Halstead Town Hall, for example, on 25 February 1864,

> He took it that Englishmen did not like America, and he believed the compliment was returned – they didn't like us (laughter); nevertheless there was nothing the Americans desired as the good-will of England. They were loud, encroaching, boastful and conceited, and they disliked us for the same reason (laughter).
> (*Halstead Times*, 27 Feb 1864)

In fact the two nations had much in common, hence their rivalry:

> Englishmen thought it their duty to Anglicize the world: the Americans were chips of the old block, and wished to American-ize the whole world (cheers). Hating each other for slight differences, and far more for resemblances, England and America ought rather to seek good living for the masses, and by good living he meant not merely beef and pudding, although they formed no unimportant part, but free commerce, free government, free religion without priestcraft, and to enjoy the life of a man and not of a brute (cheers).

He hoped America would survive the crisis. 'Loud, disagreeable, self-conceited she might be: it was the folly of youth (laughter).' America had often made him angry, but he admired her progress and dynamism.

At Leeds Mechanics' Institute, one week earlier, he had boldly denounced the Southern states: 'Their being little did not justify them, and he no more sympathized with them on this account than he would sympathize with a thief because he had fallen into the more powerful hands of the police.' Bold words in the depressed textile manufacturing areas of northern England, but he was applauded mightily. This was the conclusion of his speech 'Politics as a Daily Study for Common People' in which he showed concern for educating the masses. 'Our great national deficiency . . . was a want of education amongst our labouring people.' Everyone – women as well as men – ought to study politics, domestic and international. He added, amidst laughter, that they might even get more benefit from studying politics than reading novels. As for women,

> There used to be an idea that women should not be politicians, just as formerly it was an accepted idea that they should not read and write, and that knitting and cookery were the only essentials for ladies. From that thraldom they had escaped, and as to cooking he sometimes thought they had left it a little too far behind (laughter).   (*Leeds Mercury*, 19 Feb 1864, 7)

A woman was environed by political circumstances, and nothing could be more absurd than supposing she had no interest in politics.

Trollope advocated wider opportunities for female education and employment and was to write on jobs for them in the Post Office: 'The Young Women at the London Telegraph Office' (*Good Words*, xvii [June 1877] 377–84).

Education of the lower middle class was a special interest.[18] One of his best speeches on this topic was at the Liverpool Institute on 13 November 1873, when he presented prizes to successful candidates in entrance examinations for Oxford, Cambridge and London. He began with his usual variations on the theme of wisely used leisure and the benefits of good reading material. He recalled schoolfellows 'who never seemed to require amusement, – who were always devoted to their tasks'. He went on, 'as Jacks they were not only dull boys, but . . . as grown-up Johns they were usually duller men'. He hoped that boys in the Institute and commercial schools would go on to read poetry as well as novels.

After the usual references to the models of Dickens and Thackeray as moral benefactors (from his address on English fiction) he spoke of education in general, making a special point about popular education among the labouring population. For the latter, Forster's Education Act had already achieved much:

> None could fail to be convinced that in spite of remaining difficulties – difficulties as to secular and denominational education, and as to compulsory and voluntary education – we were, at any rate, entitled to say that we were achieving now the education of the country generally (Applause). (*Liverpool Mail*, 15 Nov 1873, 5)

His sphere of interest, however, was the education of the commercial classes undertaken by the Liverpool Institute and similar centres. The public schools with their 'fine old English names' were, he felt, despite reforms, 'still infected by the medieval conditions of the times in which they were founded'. Originally founded as charity schools, 'they were now devoted almost exclusively to the education of the rich. He was himself educated at Winchester as a charity boy (Applause)'; grateful as he was for that start in life, he declared that schools so exclusive in these days should be entirely self-supporting.

Trollope's lectures and speeches were not conspicuous for originality or brilliant execution, but he addressed issues of the day as a gentleman of his class, conservatively biased, patriotic and wholeheartedly sincere. He had little wit and no sense of the dramatic, but he carried his audience with him. He was at his best when his theme was literature, which he defended passionately. The farewell banquet to Dickens on his departure for America in November 1867 gave him the opportunity to speak with due regard of Dickens' pre-eminence (Trollope called him 'a great chieftain in literature') and with feeling for the vocation they shared. Trollope responded to the toast to literature, and, although in letters he had expressed reluctance to be present ('I am not specially in that set, but having been asked I did not like to refuse' – *L*, I, 397), he rose well to the occasion. Since what he said has not been hitherto accessible to the general reader, a summary follows.

The scene in Freemasons' Hall was resplendent, with titles of Dickens' novels in 20 arched panels, sumptuous floral displays and the flags of Britain and the United States. Over 500 guests were in the hall, with ladies in the gallery. After being received by prolonged cheering, Trollope acknowledged the chairman, Lord Lytton, and guests, and, the preamble over, he at once commended the healthy state of literature in England, denying that there was any imminent crisis to the nation's morals and well-being, as had lately been uttered by 'a great prophet among us'. This direct reference to Carlyle occasioned a tribute to the sage, whose example, Trollope said, had been 'a long life of truth and honesty' and dedicated work. However, it was Trollope's opinion that Carlyle had been carried away by 'a melancholy enthusiasm of foreboding', until he could cry nothing to his brethren but 'Woe, woe from the housetop.' Fortunately Carlyle was not present to hear Trollope's obvious imitation and quoting (doubtless amidst laughter), 'Fiction . . . O my friend! You will have to think how perilous and close a cousinship it has with lying.' Trollope thought these were harsh words indeed – 'hard words to us who do our teaching by the telling of tales instead of by the speaking of prophecies'. And, launching himself into the dramatic mode, he offered some examples to delight his listeners:

> Was Colonel Newcome – that finest gentleman of past days – was he a lie? Were the words which Jane Eyre addressed to her lover when he demanded whether she would take from him his one drop of water – a lie? Was the sermon which Dinah preached upon the green – was that a lie? (Cheers). Gentlemen, do you remember – who here does not remember – the walk which Sikes took with his dog after the murder? (Renewed cheering).

Having tactfully alluded to eminent colleagues and disposed of Carlyle, he came to the peroration:

> My belief is that we who write fiction have taught purity of life, nobility of action, and self-denial, and have taught those lessons with allurements both to the old and the young which no other teacher of the present day can reach, and which no prophet can teach (Cheers).[19]

In its way this graceful tribute to the art he served for some 40 years of extraordinary vigour and dedication is an appropriate conclusion to this essay. Few writers, indeed, have crowded so much into their working day – not to mention their leisure – as Trollope. From the time of his acceptance in the literary circle of Thackeray, the Chronology records an astonishing round of the London and provincial scene, hunting and other social pursuits, travels abroad, and a roll-call of celebrities in arts, politics, the

aristocracy and landed gentry. At his death, and on publication of
the *Autobiography*, tributes reflected the respect and affection in
which he was so widely held. A selection of those tributes is given
as Appendix C.

Major sources for the Chronology are the incomparable *Trollope:
A Commentary* by Michael Sadleir (1927), and the meticulously
researched two-volume edition of *The Letters of Anthony Trollope*,
edited by N. John Hall with the assistance of Nina Burgis (Stanford,
Calif., 1983). Three important collections of manuscript material
have been consulted for this volume: the Morris L. Parrish Collec-
tion and Robert H. Taylor Collection of Princeton University
Library; the Trollope family papers in the University of Illinois
Library; and three manuscript notebooks in the Bodleian Library,
Oxford. In such a project the obligation to past Trollope scholarship
is extensive, and I am indebted to T. H. S. Escott's *Anthony Trollope:
His Work, Associates and Literary Originals* (1913), and biographies
by R. P. and L. P. Stebbins, *The Trollopes: The Chronicle of a Writing
Family* (New York, 1945), James Pope Hennessy, *Anthony Trollope*
(1971) and C. P. Snow, *Trollope* (1975). For a number of contempor-
ary records I have had recourse to Thomas Adolphus Trollope's
What I Remember, 2 vols (1887), and F. E. Trollope's *Frances Trollope:
Her Life and Literary Work from George III to Victoria*, 2 vols (1895).
Details of Trollope's business arrangements have been alluded to
in appropriate contexts and are based on Michael Sadleir's *Trollope:
A Bibliography* (1928, supplemented 1934). Other useful biblio-
graphic information may be found in John Sutherland's *Victorian
Novelists and Publishers* (1976). Brief surveys of contemporary
opinions on Trollope's work follow details of publication, and in
this connection I have had the help of *Anthony Trollope* (Critical
Heritage), edited by Donald Smalley (1969), and David Skilton's
*Anthony Trollope and his Contemporaries: A Study in the Theory and
Conventions of Mid-Victorian Fiction* (1972). Valuable information has
also been gathered from more recent studies such as Helen
Heineman's *Mrs Trollope: The Triumphant Feminine in the Nineteenth
Century* (Athens, Ohio, 1979) and R. H. Super's *Trollope in the Post
Office* (Ann Arbor, Mich., 1981).

Dating events in Trollope's full itinerary is a hazardous business,
since, although he maintained copious records, hasty notations in
his notoriously appalling hand, studied largely on microfilm, tend
to undermine editorial confidence and must inevitably lead to
misjudgements. Where there is some uncertainty about a date,

person, place or event, it is preceded or followed by a query (the precise placing of the query depends on layout and context). While every effort has been made to verify sources, the editor regrets any misreadings from manuscript sources. Conjectural meetings based on letters and invitations for future dates have been indicated in the text. Footnotes have been replaced by explanations bracketed and placed in their context for the reader's convenience. Most sources of significant detail concerning persons known to Trollope are also supplied in the text, usually on first citation. A list of abbreviations for frequently cited works precedes the Chronology.

In addition to the work of earlier scholars already mentioned, fellow Trollopians have put me on the track of items and dates relating to Trollope's life and career. I wish to thank in particular N. John Hall for his encyclopaedic knowledge of Trollope and patient attention to my inquiries. For some details of the itineraries I am indebted to the researches of P. D. Edwards and R. B. Joyce (Australia) and J. H. Davidson (South Africa). I also acknowledge the help of D. Wainwright, Curator of the Morris L. Parrish Collection of Victorian Novelists, Princeton University Library. I wish to thank staffs of the following libraries: the University of Illinois, Boston Public Library, the University of London, the Bodleian, and the British Library and Newspaper Library. Colleagues at the University of Victoria Library, especially in its inter-library loan section, have been most helpful. I also thank the University of Victoria for research funds enabling me to undertake research for this book in London, Oxford, Princeton and Boston. Many individuals have also contributed advice and assistance. I wish to express my deepest appreciation to Sarah Harvey, whose effort digging out relevant dates and events from wide sources has frequently come to my rescue and at times restored my enthusiasm for the untiring Anthony. For her minute care over the presentation of the finished typescript and secretarial efficiency I thank Colleen Donnelly. And for his patient encouragement at various stages of the project I am indebted to the General Editor of the series, Norman Page.

Notes

1. Bradford Booth, *The Letters of Anthony Trollope* (1951) p. xxi.
2. Recounted by Cecilia Meetkerke in 'Last Reminiscences of Anthony Trollope', *Temple Bar*, LXX (Jan 1884) 130–4. This, and several following references (indicated in the text by '*I & R*'), may be found in *Trollope:*

Interviews and Recollections, ed. R. C. Terry (1987). Other abbreviated forms may be checked in the List of Abbreviations and Short Titles following.

3. The Revd Edward Bradley (1827–89), pen name 'Cuthbert Bede', author of *The Adventures of Mr Verdant Green* (1854) and other comic novels of university life.

4. Anne Isabella Thackeray (1837–1919), Thackeray's elder daughter and author of *The Story of Elizabeth* (1862) and other popular novels.

5. *E*, p. 170.

6. Henry James (1843–1916) had first-hand evidence; he was aboard the same ship, the *Bothnia*, out of New York in the rough crossing season of November 1875.

7. *H*, pp. 186, 192, 196–8, 201. Escott affirmed that in the late 1840s also there was 'regular and copious communication' between them (*Anthony Trollope*, p. 83).

8. *S*, pp. 3–4.

9. A practically verbatim record of the courtroom battle will be found in *I & R*, pp. 40–4.

10. *S*, p. 44.

11. Mary Katherine Keemle Field (1838–96), an American journalist, actress, women's rights activist, whom Trollope called 'out of my own family, my most chosen friend' (*Auto.*, p. 271).

12. The Revd William Lucas Collins (1817–87), Rector of Lowick, Northamptonshire, in the heart of the hunting country Trollope loved. While staying at Collins' home he wrote *Dr Wortle's School* (publ. 1881).

13. R. C. Terry, *Anthony Trollope: The Artist in Hiding* (1977) p. 40.

14. See Patricia Srebrnik, 'Trollope, James Virtue and *Saint Paul's Magazine*', *Nineteenth-Century Fiction*, xxxvii, no. 3 (Dec 1982) 443–63.

15. See R. H. Super, 'Trollope at the Royal Literary Fund', ibid., pp. 316–28; Bradford Booth, 'Trollope and the Royal Literary Fund', *Nineteenth-Century Fiction*, vii, no. 3 (Dec 1952) 208–16.

16. The first four listed may be found in *Four Lectures*, ed. Morris L. Parrish (privately printed, 1938; repr. 1969).

17. W. P. Frith, *My Autobiography and Reminiscences*, 3 vols (1887–8) iii, 386.

18. Enthusiasm for this sector of public education probably arose from his friendship with the Revd William Rogers (1819–96), Rector of St Botolph's, Bishopsgate, from 1863. An ardent education reformer, Rogers raised funds for a school in Cowper Street for children of clerks and tradesmen, enrolling 1000 pupils. A striking feature was its secular policy, which earned him the nickname 'Hang Theology' Rogers. A friend of Jowett and fellow member of the Athenaeum, he was just the kind of cleric Trollope liked.

19. William Charles Mark Kent, *The Dickens Dinner* (1867) pp. 24–5. Another generous tribute to Dickens was delivered at the Royal Academy's annual dinner on 29 April 1871. See David A. Roos, 'Dickens at the Royal Academy of Arts: A New Speech and Two Eulogies', *Dickensian*, lxxiii (May 1977) 104.

List of Abbreviations and Short Titles

ANZ Anthony Trollope, *Australia and New Zealand*, 2 vols (1873)

AT Anthony Trollope

Auto. Anthony Trollope, *An Autobiography* (1883), World's Classics edn (Oxford, Classics, 1961)

Comm. Michael Sadleir, *Anthony Trollope: A Commentary* (1927, rev. 1945)

E T. H. S. Escott, *Anthony Trollope: His Work, Associates and Literary Originals* (1913)

FT Frances Trollope

FT Frances Eleanor Trollope, *Frances Trollope: Her Life and Literary Work from George III to Victoria*, 2 vols (1895)

GE George Eliot

GE *The George Eliot Letters*, ed. G. S. Haight, 9 vols (New Haven, Conn., 1954–78)

GHL George Henry Lewes

H Helen Heineman, *Mrs Trollope: The Triumphant Feminine in the Nineteenth Century* (Athens, Ohio, 1979)

I & R *Anthony Trollope: Interviews and Recollections*, ed. R. C. Terry (1987)

L *The Letters of Anthony Trollope*, ed. N. John Hall with the assistance of Nina Burgis, 2 vols (Stanford, Calif., 1983)

S R. H. Super, *Trollope in the Post Office* (Ann Arbor, Mich., 1981)

SA Anthony Trollope, *South Africa*, 2 vols (1878)

TAT Thomas Adolphus Trollope

WIR Thomas Adolphus Trollope, *What I Remember*, 2 vols (1887)

A Trollope Chronology

1802–1833

We know very little of AT's childhood, for which the major sources are still *An Autobiography* (published posthumously 1883) and family reminiscences by TAT (*WIR*) and FT (*FT*). The story of AT's wretched boyhood recounted by Sadleir (*Comm.*) may be supplemented by other biographical accounts in Escott (*E*), Stebbins, Pope Hennessy and Snow (see Introduction). Valuable material, particularly about AT and his mother, may be found in Heineman's biography of FT (*H*).

Anthony Trollope's mother was Frances Milton (1779–1863), daughter of the Revd William Milton (1742–1824), Vicar of Heckfield, near Reading, Berkshire. She was born in 1779, one of four children, and as a girl manifested the lively spirit that was to sustain her through much toil and unhappiness in later life. In 1808 her brother Henry Milton (1784?–1850) introduced her to Thomas Anthony Trollope (1774–1835), a barrister, aged 34, whom she married after a year of sedate courtship. They set up house at 16 Keppel Street, Bloomsbury, London, naming their first son Thomas Adolphus, the second name complimenting a wealthy kinsman from whom Trollope had expectations of fortune. His uncle Adolphus Meetkerke (1819–79) owned an estate called Julians, near Royston, Hertfordshire, and on all sides his nephew was looked upon as his heir. When Trollope built a lavish house at Harrow on farmland leased from Lord Northwick and took to farming (the house was named 'Julians'), it was in keen anticipation of Uncle Adolphus's fortune – an expectation cruelly disappointed in the event, as Adolphus married and had heirs of his own.

The blow was bravely borne, but Thomas Anthony became from this time increasingly embittered and cantankerous – a good man, still, his elder son insisted, but steadily less comfortable to be around. Nor was his temper improved by heavy doses of calomel (which may have hastened his death) to assuage blinding headaches. Frances, on the other hand, was opposite in nature – sanguine, volatile and determined to hold the family together. Her bazaar in Cincinnati selling trinkets from home was a bold move, however impractical, but her truly heroic role was played later when amidst illness and death she chained herself to a routine of writing, beginning with *The Domestic Manners of the Americans* (1832). No tribute surpasses that of Trollope's first biographer, Michael Sadleir, who describes her in the period following the family's hasty escape from creditors to the town of Bruges as manager, nurse, provider of meals and solitary breadwinner, grinding out fashionable novels – 'the epic, surely the unique, achievement of this battered but indomitable woman' (*Comm.*, p. 85).

The Trollopes had seven children: Thomas Adolphus (1810–92), Henry (1811–34), Arthur William (1812–24), Emily (b. and d. 9 Dec 1813), Anthony (1815–82), Cecilia (1816–49) and a second Emily (1818–36).

1802	(14 Nov) Mary Mitford meets Frances Milton among guests at the estate of Lord Rivers in Heckfield, and finds her 'a very lively, pleasant young woman'.

1803	Frances Milton joins her brother Henry, a clerk at the War Office, in London. She enjoys theatres, museums and society.

1808	(Summer) Henry Milton introduces her to Thomas Anthony Trollope, a barrister of Lincoln's Inn.

1809	(23 May) Marriage of Frances Milton and Thomas Anthony Trollope. They settle at 16 Keppel Street, Bloomsbury, a locality 'at that time inhabited by the professional classes' (*WIR*, i, 2). Despite their modest resources, the establishment includes a liveried footman.

1810	(29 Apr) Birth of Thomas Adolphus Trollope (d. 1892). 'Everybody exclaims that my darling is the loveliest creature they ever beheld' (*H*, p. 17).

(Summer) Thomas Anthony begins looking for a farm.

1813	(Summer) He finds Illot's Farm, 160 acres near Harrow, and decides to take a lease from Lord Northwick.

(Sep) Takes possession of Illot's Farm and installs a bailiff and tenant. AT is to write of the farm as 'the grave of all my father's hopes, ambition, and prosperity, the cause of my mother's sufferings, and of those of her children, and perhaps the director of her destiny and of ours' (*Auto.*, p. 2). His brother concurred: 'The move to Harrow was as infelicitous a step in the economic point of view as it was inefficacious as a measure of health' (*WIR*, I, 57).

1815 (Mon 24 Apr) Birth of Anthony Trollope (d. 1882).
(18 May) AT baptised at St George's, Bloomsbury.
Late this year, the family moves to Harrow.

1816 Birth of Cecilia Frances Trollope (d. 1849).

1818 Thomas Anthony embarks on building a lavish house, spending large sums on roadways, fences and drainage improvements. FT enthusiastically joins in plans for landscaping. The completed house is christened 'Julians', after the estate of Trollope's uncle Adolphus Meetkerke, whose wealth he expects to inherit. Soon after the house is built, Meetkerke marries, ending all hopes of an inheritance.
Also this year, Emily Trollope born (d. 1836).

1819 (2 May) Charles Merivale (1808–93) notes a party with the Trollopes at which the children play 'Commerce'. Thomas Anthony quotes Greek poets and FT listens with admiration to Herman Merivale (1806–74) reciting Dante. [Merivale, later Under-Secretary for India, contributor to *Fortnightly Review*.]

1820 TAT begins his schooling at Winchester.
(12 Feb) Still bent on improving Julians, now leased to Harrow's vicar, the Revd John William Cunningham, the Trollopes decide to return to Illot's Farm, which they now bravely call 'Julians Hill'. Enlargements and improvements are embarked upon. [The drawing of it executed by J. E. Millais in 1861 becomes the frontispiece to *Orley Farm*.]

1823–5 (Summer) AT attends Harrow School as a day boy.

1823 FT writes 'Salmagundi Aliena', attacking Cunningham and other local worthies who had objected to Byron raising a tablet in Harrow to his illegitimate daughter Allegra (d. Apr 1822).
(Late Aug) The Trollopes travel to France for a sightseeing

holiday. Washington Irving (1783–1859) later records meeting the couple as 'Mrs Trollop [sic] & husband'. General Lafayette remarks her 'agreeable and amiable qualities'.

1825–7 AT attends a private school at Sunbury, Middlesex, conducted by Arthur Drury. Although always without pocket money, he lives 'more nearly on terms of equality with other boys than at any other period' (*Auto.*, p. 4).

1826 (Sep) FT hears from her friend Frances Wright about progress of her utopian community at Nashoba, Tennessee. [Frances Wright (1795–1852) an idealistic feminist, was author of *Views of Society and Manners in America during the years 1818–19–20*, published in 1821.]

(Oct) Amateur theatricals at Julians Hill. Thomas Anthony notes, 'Steven is a good prompter, and thunders capitally; we have not tried our lightning yet.' On another occasion the drawing room is transformed for a performance of *Les Femmes savantes* (*FT*, ɪ, 89).

1827 (11 Apr) FT writes to TAT that it will be essential to keep Anthony up to the mark at Winchester (see next entry) if he is to get to New College, Oxford. 'As far as Anthony is concerned this must very much depend on you. I dare say you will often find him idle and plaguing enough. But remember, dear Tom, that, in a family like ours, *everything* gained by one is felt personally and individually by all' (*FT*, ɪ, 95). Tom apparently took his responsibilities seriously: 'he was', wrote AT later, 'of all my foes the worst . . . as a part of his daily exercise, he thrashed me with a big stick' (*Auto.*, p. 7).

(14 Apr) AT is admitted to Winchester College, where he remains until summer 1830.

(4 Nov) FT sails to America with Henry, Cecilia and Emily, intent on visiting Nashoba. She opens a bazaar in Cincinnati, largely at her husband's instigation, selling 'pincushions, pepper-boxes, and pocket-knives'. The venture is disastrous: within six months the building is put into receivership.

1828 (Sep) Thomas Anthony travels to America with TAT.

1829 (Mar) He returns to England and moves to Harrow Weald 'to live at a wretched tumble-down farmhouse . . . in danger of falling into the neighbouring horse-pond'. AT relieves his solitude 'in the kitchen, making innocent love to the bailiff's daughter'. He looks back later on this period as the worst: 'The indignities I endured are not to be described. As I look back it seems to me that all hands were turned against me, – those of masters as well as boys' (*Auto.*, pp. 9–10).

1830 (19 Apr) Henry arrives in England. Deposited by the Liverpool coach in London and without funds, he has to walk the 16 miles home.

(Summer) FT writes to TAT (then at Oxford) from Cincinnati, '*Everything* from the time you left us, went wrong. . . . Poor Cecilia is literally without shoes, and I mean to sell one or two small articles tomorrow to procure some for her, and for Emily. I sit still and write, write, write, – so old shoes last me a long time. . . . My poor dear Anthony will have outgrown our recollection! Tell him not to outgrow his affection for us. No day passes, – hardly an hour – without our talking of you all' (*FT*, ɪ, 130–1).

Also this summer, AT is removed from Winchester, all hopes of following his father to New College, Oxford, at an end. [TAT likewise did not fulfil his father's academic ambitions, but was educated at Alban Hall.]

(Dec) After a disastrous hay crop Thomas Anthony receives an ultimatum from Lord Northwick that, unless rent arrears are paid in five days, household goods will be seized. He settles by instalments.

(1830?) During vacation TAT arrives from Oxford and accompanies AT to Vauxhall to see the fireworks. With two shillings to spend, they walk 14 miles, arriving in the evening. AT dances all night and then they walk home 'without having touched bite or sup!' (*WIR*, ɪ, 240).

1831 (Jan) Sent again to Harrow School, a daily walk of 12 miles. 'He gave no sign of promise whatever, was always in the lowest part of the form, and was regarded by masters and by boys as an incorrigible dunce' (*Sir William Gregory, KCMG: An Autobiography*, ed. Lady Gregory [1894] p. 35).

(5 Aug) FT arrives from America and finds the family finances in total disarray, largely through annual losses on the Harrow farm.

(Sep) Manuscript of FT's American tour is praised by Captain Basil Hall. A room set aside in the Harrow Weald farm for her writing is christened 'The Sacred Den of Harrow'. Her nickname later becomes 'Old Mother Vinegar' (*Comm.*, p. 80). Thomas Anthony buries himself in research for an ecclesiastical encyclopaedia, but his violent scenes with his children cause FT much anxiety. 'So shaken and agitated', she has occasional resource to a dose of laudanum to secure a night's rest (*H*, p. 78).

Also during this year, Henry Stuart Russell (1819–89) is AT's fag at Harrow and witnesses a great fight between AT and another boy. The opponent is so heavily beaten that he has to go home. Judge Thomas Henry Baylis (1817–1908), a contemporary at Harrow, declares although home boarders were often bullied, AT, 'being big and powerful, got off easily'.

1832 TAT records in his diary, 'Went to town yesterday, and among other commissions bought a couple of single-sticks with strong basket handles. Anthony much approves of them, and this morning we had a bout with them. One of the sticks bought yesterday soon broke, and we supplied its place by a tremendous blackthorn. Neither of us left the arena without a fair share of rather severe wales; but Anthony is far my superior in quickness and adroitness, and perhaps in bearing pain too. I fear he is likely to remain so in the first two, but in the third I am determined he shall not' (*WIR*, I, 226).

(19 Mar) Publication of FT's *The Domestic Manners of the Americans*; it soon exhausts its first edition. Debts are paid and the family living standard improves; purchases include coal, candles, furniture, a cow, and malt for brewing.

(Summer) FT goes to London to promote her book and is delighted to find everyone 'talking Yankee talk' (*H*, p. 102).

(Sep) The Trollope family move back to Julians Hill. AT's schooling goes on 'under somewhat improved circumstances' (*Auto.*, p. 14).

1833 AT tries unsuccessfully to gain a scholarship to Trinity College, Oxford (*Comm.*, p. 80). [AT also records two attempts for a sizarship at Clare Hall (*Auto.*, p. 15).]

(Oct) Thomas Anthony unable to meet his monthly bills. Lord Northwick threatens legal action.

(Dec) He scrapes together what money he can but manages only £25 as payment. Northwick's agent calls on Boxing Day and finds Thomas Anthony has taken to his bed. For the first time FT learns of large arrears for which Lord Northwick is demanding payment. The agent reports, 'He don't appear to me to have but very little stock dead or alive . . . .' Final collapse of Cincinnati venture and loss of remaining capital (*H*, p. 113).

1834–1840

The circumstances of AT's entry into the General Post Office, amusingly told in the *Auto.*, are paralleled in his fictional account of Charley Tudor's entry to the Civil Service in *The Three Clerks* (ch. 2). AT's first seven years of official life, he confesses, 'were neither creditable to myself nor useful to the public service' (*Auto.*, p. 37), but a transfer to the Central District of Ireland in 1841 as surveyor's clerk brought about a miraculous transformation. From an unpunctual, quarrelsome, insubordinate hobbledehoy 'always on the eve of being dismissed' (*Auto.*, p. 39), he was to become 'one of the most efficient and valuable officers in the Post Office' (*WIR*, I, 259). His initial appointment arose from his mother's friends the Freelings, but Sir Francis Freeling, the Secretary, was replaced by Lt-Col. William Leader Maberly, an irascible gentleman, with whom AT was soon in conflict. Antagonistic to authority and again conscious of his isolation, AT floundered from one scrape to another, beset by duns, twice taken up for debt, and once berated by a woman in the office demanding, 'Anthony Trollope, when are you going to marry my daughter?' (*Auto.*, p. 41). He became convinced that his life was heading 'downwards to the lowest pits' (*Auto.*, p. 49). But soon after leaving England he pulled himself together, began to enjoy his work, made friends among his Irish hosts, took up hunting, married, started a family, and found the impetus for a first novel. Recent scholarship has added to our knowledge of those early years, notably through the work of R. H. Super (*S*) and N. John Hall (*L*).

1834 (Spring) FT's brother, Henry Milton, informs her that title to her husband's London property is insecure, and that her marriage settlement had been improperly registered. She is concerned about her family's health. 'For about ten days we were very seriously alarmed for Anthony – and since that more seriously still for my poor Henry . . .' (*H*, p. 111).

(Apr) Lord Northwick's agent reports, 'I think the most prudent course to pursue will be to seize at the proper time and sell the present growing crops and permit Mr Trollope to let his farm from Michaelmas next by which means I should hope your lordship will realize all that is and will then be due to him' (*H*, p. 114).

Also in April, AT leaves Harrow. 'From the first to the last there was nothing satisfactory in my school career, – except the way in which I licked the boy who had to be taken home to be cured' (*Auto.*, p. 16). Sir William Gregory (1817–92), who had sat next to him at school, would recall, 'He was a big boy, older than the rest of the form, and without exception the most slovenly and dirty boy I ever met. . . . His exercises were a mass of blots and smudges. . . . I avoided him, for he was rude and uncouth, but I thought him an honest, brave fellow. His faults were external; all the rest of him was right enough' (Gregory, *An Autobiography*, p. 35).

(18 Apr) AT drives his father in the family gig to board a boat for Ostend before bailiffs descend on Julians Hill. FT prudently has her new furniture carried to a neighbour, Colonel Grant, for safe keeping. In the late 1860s AT would show Frith's daughter 'with many chuckles where there had been a hole in the hedge' through which he and his sisters had smuggled china and silver. '. . . between us we cheated the creditors to the extent of our powers, amidst the anathemas, but goodhumoured abstinence from personal violence of the men in charge of the property' (*Auto.*, p. 23).

(May) The Trollopes settle in a large house, the Château d'Hondt, at Bruges. 'There were six of us went into this new banishment. My brother Henry had left Cambridge and was ill [then recuperating in Devon]. And though as yet we hardly told each other that it was so, we began to feel that that desolating fiend, consumption, was among us. . . . My elder sister and I were in good health, but I was an idle, desolate hanger-on, that most hopeless of human beings, a hobbledehoy of nineteen, without any idea of a career, a profession, or a trade' (*Auto.*, p. 24).

(Summer) Becomes for six weeks a classical usher at William Drury's school at Brussels.

(Autumn) Arriving at Bruges from Brussels, AT learns of Emily's failing health. Cecilia has been sent to her uncle Henry's at Pinner, near Harrow, to avoid infection. FT is now nursing three invalids and writing far into the night. 'The doctor's vial and the ink-bottle held equal places in mother's rooms. I have written many novels under many circumstances; but I doubt whether I could write one when my whole heart was by the bedside of a dying son' (*Auto.*, pp. 24–5).

(2 Nov) Of AT's imminent postal appointment FT writes, 'I am happier in receiving this news than I thought anything just now could make me' (*FT*, I, 227).

(4 Nov) AT enters the General Post Office as a junior clerk at St Martin's le Grand at a salary of £90 a year, thanks to his mother's friendship with Mrs Clayton Freeling, daughter-in-law of the Secretary, Sir Francis Freeling (1764–1836). He briefly shares his brother's lodgings in Little Marlborough Street, and then moves to 22 Northumberland Street, Marylebone, overlooking the Workhouse – 'a most dreary abode' (*Auto.*, p. 46).

(23 Dec) Henry Trollope dies. FT writes to TAT, 'I need the comfort of your presence' (*FT*, I, 228).

1835 (20 Jan) FT appeals to John Murray (1778–1843), publisher, for some literary work for AT. 'He would gladly occupy the hours of his evening in some profitable employment. He is a good scholar, and, as I believe your friend Henry Drury [AT's tutor at Harrow School] will allow, has very good abilities. It has been suggested to him that he might possibly find employment either by correcting the press, or in some other occupation of this kind, and I should be very grateful if you could help him in obtaining such' (*L*, I, 3).

(Aug) AT begins a Commonplace Book [now in the Beinecke Library at Yale] maintained over five years and reflecting his reading and literary interests. Comments on novels by the author of *Pelham*, Bulwer-Lytton (1803–73), John Galt, G. P. R. James. A favourite work is Henry Taylor's *Philip Van Artevelde*. [Earlier literary leanings were manifested in extensive notes to a volume of Edmund Burke and in 1834 to a poem of his mother's.]

(Oct) On the way to their father's deathbed in Bruges, TAT visits AT in his lodgings in Northumberland Street.

(23 Oct) AT's father dies. 'I sometimes look back, meditating for hours together, on his adverse fate. . . . The touch of his hand seemed to create failure. . . . We were all estranged from him, and yet I believe he would have given his heart's blood for any of us. His life as I knew it was one long tragedy' (*Auto.*, p. 27).

1836 (Jan) FT resides at Hadley, Hertfordshire; AT visits her several times.

(12 Feb) Death of Emily. AT writes to TAT, 'It is all over! Poor Emily breathed her last this morning. She died without any pain, and without a struggle. Her little strength had been gradually declining, and her breath left her without the slightest convulsion, or making any change in her features or face' (*L*, I, 2).

1837 (Feb–Mar) AT busies himself with publishers over his mother's books *Belgium and Western Germany in 1833* and *Vienna and the Austrians*.

(20 Feb) Conveys a message from FT to Richard Bentley (1794–1871).

1838 (12 Jan) FT proposes to move from Hadley: 'a change which both Anthony's occupations and mine renders desirable, albeit I love my pretty cottage here . . . in truth four hours out of every day is too much for Anthony to pass in, or on, a coach, which is what he now does' (*H*, p. 154).

(Summer) FT, AT, TAT and Cecilia move to 20 York Street, Portman Square. Proud of his mother's success with her travel book *Paris and the Parisians in 1835*, AT writes to TAT, 'No work of hers was ever abused so much – or sold so fast – or praised in the periodicals so little – especially by her own party' (*L*, I, 2).

(Dec) Fails to copy and dispatch important letters. His superior notes, 'I have observed with much regret an habitual carelessness on the part of this Officer' (*S*, p. 4).

1839 (11 Feb) Cecilia Trollope marries John Tilley (1813–98), junior clerk in the Post Office with AT until he became a surveyor in 1838. [He was promoted Assistant Secretary (1848) and Secretary (1864). He retired from the Postal Service in 1880 and was created KCB the same year.] After the wedding, AT together with FT and TAT visit the Grants, old friends from Harrow days.

(28 Mar?) Alexander Donnadieu, musician and autograph dealer, dines at York Street.

(Apr) AT overstays a weekend leave by half a day but satisfactorily explains his absence.

(May) Falls seriously behind in his work; is ordered to make up time lost and loses seniority which would have entitled him to the next promotion. The Secretary, Lt-Col. Maberly, notes, 'I regret to be compelled to make such a proposition but Mr Trollope is without excuse, as he has good abilities & as this neglect, which has undoubtedly brought the Dept. into discredit (for some of the Cases are most gross) is entirely produced by the want of proper attention to his duty' (S, p. 4). [William Leader Maberly (1798–1885) was Secretary of the Post Office, 1836–54.]

(Sep) After visiting the Tilleys in Penrith, FT decides to move to the Lake District.

(26 Sep) FT writes to a friend about a 'promise of long-standing' to AT, whose official duties had prevented 'his sharing the travelling delights of his errant family'. The promise was of a trip to Paris, and she hoped her son would be allowed several weeks leave, 'which will give him, perhaps the only opportunity he may have of seeing *la belle ville*' (H, p. 192).

(Late in year) Active on his mother's behalf, AT sometimes collects her payments from publishers. FT asks Henry Colburn (?–1855) on one occasion to have payments ready early in the day 'in order to permit [Anthony] getting to his office at the usual time' (H, p. 186).

(4 Dec) FT and AT arrive in Boulogne at the start of their holiday in Paris. She notes how much her son enjoyed 'going to so many good parties' (FT, i, 313).

1840 (2 July) AT is stricken by a mysterious illness. FT writes to Lady Lytton (1802–82) that he 'lies in a state that defies the views of his physicians as effectually as it puzzles my ignorance. . . . He is frightfully reduced in size and strength. . . . Day by day I lose hope, and so, I am quite sure, do his physicians; we have had three consultations, but nothing prescribed relieves him, nor has any light been thrown on the nature of his complaint' (H, pp. 197–8). In despair FT calls in Dr Elliotson, a practitioner of mesmerism, who brings the Okey sisters to AT's bedside. [Under mesmeric influence the girls were in the habit of declaring that they saw Jack by the bedside of patients about to die.] TAT records that one of them saw Jack by his brother's side, but only up to his knee. Therefore he would recover (WIR, i, 370).

(9 July) AT much improved, although his progress is extremely slow.

(Nov) Junior clerks blamed for not following instructions for reporting expenditures to the Accountant-General; AT found par-

ticularly remiss. [In Ireland he keeps meticulous records, now in
the Morris L. Parrish Collection, Princeton University Library.]

1841–1847

1841   (Feb) AT on the carpet again for failing to follow correct
procedures concerning an Irish £3 note found improperly enclosed
in a newspaper. The money is lost. Ordered to make good AT
offers an explanation and is not made to pay up.

(29 July) Appointed surveyor's clerk in the Central District of
Ireland. Among his last brushes with London authority is a violent
quarrel with a fellow clerk reported to the Postmaster-General. AT
is required to write a letter of apology: 'any refusal on his part to
give it will be at his peril' (*S*, p. 10). [For accounts of some of his
early experiences in Ireland see *I & R*, pp. 31–45.]

(15 Sep) Arrives in Dublin and passes the night at a dirty hotel
where he has dinner and whisky punch.

(16 Sep) Reports to Secretary of the Irish Post Office and learns
that Lt-Col. Maberly had sent a report of his bad character. The
officer declares, 'I shall judge you by your own merits' (*Auto.*,
p. 54).

(19 Sep) Reaches Banagher, Co. Offaly, headquarters of the
Central District. His duties consist largely of assisting the Surveyor
in dealing with complaints, organising deliveries, and finding ways
to improve the postal service. He buys a horse and takes up riding
to hounds.

(1 Nov) Postmaster of Oranmore, Co. Galway, dismissed for
faulty accounting after AT's investigations.

1842   (9 July) On duty at the seaside resort of Kingstown (Dun
Laoghaire), outside Dublin, where he remains for two weeks.
Makes acquaintance of Edward Heseltine, Rotherham agent of the
Sheffield and Rotherham Banking Company. Meets Heseltine's
daughter, Rose.

(Mid-Aug) Returns for fortnight's holiday to Kingstown. Application for two weeks' further leave granted. Visits FT's new home
in Penrith, Cumberland, which she had occupied the previous
month. TAT travels to Ireland and finds his brother a changed
man. They ride together and walk over the mountains above the
Killeries. 'We returned wet to the skin to "Joyce's Inn", and dined

on roast goose and whisky punch, wrapped in our blankets like Roman senators' (*WIR*, I, 76). They also attend an uproarious election meeting at which the platform gives way, and they rescue a priest in the commotion.

1843 (22 Aug–15 Nov) At Drumsna, Co. Leitrim. Out walking one day with his friend John Merivale (1815–86), he comes upon a ruined house. 'It was one of the most melancholy spots I ever visited. . . . We wandered about the place . . . and while I was still among the ruined walls and decayed beams I fabricated the plot of *The Macdermots of Ballycloran*' (*Auto.*, p. 60). While at Drumsna he is sent to investigate irregularities in the post office managed by William Allen. After a weary journey he puts up at a small inn. During the night an intruder approaches his bed. He grapples with him and the man falls down the stairs. He turns out to be the parish priest. [The incident inspires AT's short story 'Father Giles of Ballymoy', published in *Lotta Schmidt and Other Stories* (1867).]

(13 Sep) Begins *The Macdermots of Ballycloran*.

1844 (Spring) Announces engagement to Rose Heseltine (1821?–1917).

(May) FT returns from Florence.

(11 June) AT marries Rose at the parish church in Rotherham: 'and perhaps I ought to name that happy day as the commencement of my better life' (*Auto.*, p. 58). FT gets on well with Rose, who recalls their early acquaintance with the evident relief of an approved daughter-in-law. 'She rose very early and made her own tea, the fire having been prepared over night – (on one occasion I remember her bringing me a cup of tea to my room, because she thought I had caught cold during a wet walk in the mountains) – then sat at her writing-table until the allotted task of so many pages was completed; and was usually on the lawn before the family breakfast-bell rang, having filled her basket with cuttings from the rosebushes for the table and drawing-room decorations' (*H*, p. 226).

(2 Aug) The Trollopes travel to Banagher, their arrival enlivened by their conveyance running into the Shannon canal.

(7 Aug) AT is working on his Irish novel. A brief flurry occurs when it is misplaced. FT learns from Rose that it is safe, and writes from Teignmouth, Devon, 'I rejoice to hear that Anthony's

manuscript is found, and I trust that he will lose no *idle* time, but give all he can, without breaking in upon his professional labours, to finish it' (*H*, p. 226).

(27 Aug) Sent as surveyor's clerk to the Southern District of Ireland, AT takes lodgings at Clonmel, Co. Tipperary, a sporting centre and home of the Tipperary Foxhounds.

(Winter) FT travels to Florence, where she seriously considers settling.

1845 (27 Feb–17 June) Postal duties at Milltown Malbay, Co. Clare.

(June?) The couple join FT visiting the Tilleys in Penrith [John Tilley is Surveyor of the Northern District of England].

(July) Finishes *The Macdermots of Ballycloran*. He entrusts completed manuscript to FT, who undertakes to help find a publisher. She agrees not to look at the work beforehand.

(Sep) FT and TAT establish new quarters in the Via del Giglio, Florence, entertaining a great deal in the ensuing months.

(24 Sep–31 Oct) At Kilkenny.

(2 Nov–21 Feb 1846) At Fermoy, Co. Cork.

1846 (13 Mar) Birth of Henry Merivale Trollope (d. 1926).

(9 May–21 Sep) Postal work throughout the Southern District.

(Aug) FT writes to Cecilia Tilley, 'I have seen [Thomas Cautley] Newby [1798?–1882] about Anthony's book. . . . He says that he thinks it very cleverly written, but that Irish stories are very unpopular' (*Comm.*, p. 141).

(14–16 Sep) Back in Ireland. Visits Glengariff and Killarney, Co. Kerry, with the Sankeys [family of Matthew Villiers Sankey of Coolmore House, Co. Tipperary].

1846–7 Writes *The Kellys and the O'Kellys* (published by Henry Colburn, 27 June 1848).

1847 (Jan) First meeting of the Brownings with FT. Robert begs Elizabeth not to receive 'that vulgar, pushing woman'. Both grow to like her.

(Mar) *The Macdermots* published by Newby on the half-profits-after-expenses system. [AT claimed it went virtually unnoticed, but there were several reviews and they were not unfavourable. It is hard to believe he was unaware that the *Spectator*, for example, found it in some ways superior to his famous mother's work, with 'less of forced continuance in the management of his story, than the fluent lady has ever displayed' (*Spectator*, xx [8 May 1847] 449). Still, AT maintained, 'It is probable that he [Newby] did not sell fifty copies' (*Auto.*, p. 64).]

(Sep) Cecilia, in Florence suffering from tuberculosis, looks 'very pale and ill, and evidently very weak'. She is moved to Rome by her mother for the winter.

(27 Sep) Birth of Frederic James Anthony Trollope (d. 1910).

(Nov) At Tralee, Co. Kerry, AT detects a young assistant postmistress stealing from the mails.

1848

Spring AT reassures his mother that revolutionary troubles were not likely to spread from Europe: 'Here in Ireland the meaning of the word Communism – or even social revolution – is not understood. The people have not the remotest notion of attempting to improve their worldly condition by making the difference between the employer and the employed less marked. Revolution here means a row' (*L*, I, 17).

3 April TAT marries the poet Theodosia Garrow (1825–65).

May Cecilia returns to England from Italy, all hopes of a cure at an end.

September AT moves to Mallow, Co. Cork, where hunting is even better than at Clonmel.

11 October Sidney Herbert describes to a friend how AT, when a fellow Harrow pupil, claimed that his ancestor, Tallyhosier the Norman, came over with William the Conqueror. Out hunting one day, he killed three wolves, and thence came the name 'troisloup', which became 'Trollope' (Lord Malmesbury, *Memoirs of an Ex-Minister* [1884] I, 234).

11 November Henry Colburn informs AT that *The Kellys* has lost money: 'it is impossible for me to give any encouragement to you to proceed in novel-writing'. [The critical response to his second novel, which was generally well received for its robust comedy, may be summed up by the comment that it was 'remarkably easy to read' (*Sharpe's London Magazine*, vii [Aug 1848] 118–21). *The Times* praised 'a native humour and a bold reality in the delineation of the characters' (7 Sep 1848, p. 6). Sales, however, reached only 140 copies.]

December   AT is embroiled in a quarrel with a mail guard whom he tries to bar from the post office at Fermoy. Lt-Col. Maberly advises the guard that superior officers must be treated with becoming deference. AT is warned to be more considerate to those under him.

Also this year, AT begins a historical novel, *La Vendée*, a tale of the French Revolution. The novel is completed in 1849.

1849

February   Hearing that Cecilia is dying, AT rushes to Kensington from Ireland.

10 March   FT arrives from Italy to be with Cecilia, 'exhausted, but grateful to find she had not been too late' (*H*, p. 235).

4 April   Death of Cecilia.

7 April   AT writes to John Tilley, 'I sometimes feel that I led you into more sorrow than happiness in taking you to Hadley [where he met Cecilia]' (*L*, i, 19).

20 April   FT writes to Rose, 'I am very glad that my dear Anthony saw her [Cecilia] on her death bed – The impression left on his mind, however painful at the moment of receiving it, will remain with him for ever more as consolation, than sorrow' (*L*, i, 19).

July   The Trollopes take their niece, Edith Tilley, to live with them at Mallow. [She remains with them until 1850.]

2 July   AT's nephew Arthur Tilley dies. FT joins AT at Mallow, where Rose takes her on walking tours. 'We took her to Killarney, with which she was enchanted. . . . She walked through the gap of Dunlo as easily as if she had been twenty-nine instead of sixty-nine [in fact seventy]' (*FT*, II, 161).

25 July   AT appears at Kerry Summer Assizes at Tralee in the case of Mary O'Reilly, assistant postmistress, charged with stealing a letter containing a sovereign. AT's evidence is crucial, since he had tracked down the offender by means of a marked coin. He faces cross-examination by the redoubtable advocate Isaac Butt (1813–79).

28 July   The *Kerry Evening Post* carries a lengthy report of the case, showing how AT rallied his cross-examiner and kept his head.

15 August   Recalling her visit to Mallow, FT writes to Rose from Charmouth, Dorset, saying how much 'her Irish excursion, and Anthony's wife and children had revived her spirits'. She missed new-laid eggs, salmon curry, Irish potatoes, a little porter, 'not to mention a few other trifles all singularly beneficial . . . since we left your hospitable domicile' (*L*, I, 19).

25 August   AT contributes the first of a series of letters to the *Examiner* on the state of the poor in Ireland. [Six more letters are published between 30 Mar and 15 June 1850.]

1850

16 January   Death of FT's brother, Henry Milton, senior official at the War Office. AT interrupts work on a guide book to Ireland which he hoped John Murray would publish. [After nine months 'it was returned without a word, in answer to a very angry letter from myself' (*Auto.*, pp. 79–80).]

15 February   Agreement with Henry Colburn for *La Vendée* guarantees £20 down and £30 more when sales reach £350. AT receives his downpayment and nothing further. [*La Vendée* was published in June. It was less noticed than its two predecessors, but the few reviews it did get praised it for creating character.]

March TAT and Theo buy a house in Florence and call it the Villino Trollope.

?May Anticipating the Great Exhibition (1851), AT tells his mother he means to exhibit four three-volume novels – 'all failures – which I look on as a great proof of industry at any rate' (*L*, ɪ, 22).

18 June Writes a comedy, *The Noble Jilt*. [It is to provide the plot of *Can You Forgive Her?*] The actor manager George Bartley responds that AT has written a five-act play without a hero.

1851

Early this year, AT writes to FT that he has bought Carlyle's *Latter-Day Pamphlets*, which he considers a waste of money: 'I look upon him as a man who was always in danger of going mad in literature, and who has now done so. I used to swear by some of his earlier works. But to my taste his writings have lost their pith and humour, while they have become stranger, and more uncouth, than ever' (*L*, ɪ, 29). [Four years later he wrote a polemical work, *The New Zealander*, in very Carlylean terms.]

March Writing to his brother, AT says he cares little for the Great Exhibition other than the building 'and my wife's piece of work which is in it' (Rose had submitted an embroidered screen which won a prize). He congratulates TAT on completing alterations to the 'Villino Trollope', Florence, bought earlier in the year. [Here TAT and his mother established a favourite meeting place of British society.]

May The *Dublin University Magazine* publishes AT's review of the first two volumes of Charles Merivale's *The History of the Romans under the Empire*. His preparation for this project encourages 'a taste generally for Latin literature, which has been one of the chief delights of my later life' (*Auto.*, p. 87). [AT's reviews of Merivale's three further volumes also appeared in *Dublin University Magazine*, July 1856.]

1 August Sails from Cork to Bristol to assist in reorganising rural posts in south-west England at the request of Rowland Hill (1795–

1879), Secretary to the Postmaster-General. The job 'so completely absorbed my time that I was able to write nothing' (*Auto.*, p. 75).

September Writes from Exeter to TAT saying he has 'such very heavy work on hand' and asking him to visit. 'You would, moreover, see Rose and Harry, who are with me. I should much like you to see little Harry' (*L*, p. 27).

October AT begins extensive checking of rural posts. 'I spent two of the happiest years of my life at the task. . . . I began in Devonshire; and visited, I think I may say, every nook in that county, in Cornwall, Somersetshire, the greater part of Dorsetshire [and several more English counties]. It is amusing to watch how a passion will grow upon a man. During those two years it was the ambition of my life to cover the country with rural letter-carriers' (*Auto.*, pp. 76–7). [For accounts of AT in the west of England see *I & R*, pp. 45–9.]

4–24 November Travels to Channel Islands as part of his western mission. His report contains a special recommendation: 'I believe that a plan has obtained in France of fitting up letter boxes in posts fixed at the road side, and it may perhaps be thought adviseable to try the operation of this system in St Heliers [*sic*]. . . . I think that the public may safely be invited to use such boxes for depositing their letters' (*S*, p. 26). [Sketches were made, an iron founder brought in, and seven pillar boxes were produced, four for Jersey and three for Guernsey.]

21 December Returns to southern Ireland (until 11 Mar 1852) at the urgent request of his superior, but his valuable service revising rural posts in England prompts Hill to have him perform the same task in Wales.

1852

In the course of his long stay in England and Wales, AT moves his family to a variety of lodgings, in Exeter, Bristol, Carmarthen, Cheltenham and Worcester.

11 March Continues mission in west of England and Wales. Comments to TAT during this month on a hectic schedule, 'I seem to be living away at a perpetual gallop. I wish I could make the pace a little slower' (*L*, i, 30).

Late May In Salisbury, idea for *The Warden* comes to him as he wanders 'round the purlieus of the cathedral . . . from whence came that series of novels of which Barchester, with its bishops, deans, and archdeacons, was the central site' (*Auto.*, p. 80).

8 June At Budleigh Salterton, Devon, calls on the Revd Hay Sweet Escott, father of T. H. S. Escott (1850–1924), who would become his first biographer. [Recalling what must have been a later visit, since it occurred after publication of *The Warden*, Escott noted that the guest 'seemingly added to his large dimension by a shaggy overcoat, or it may have been a large double-breasted pea-jacket, making him look like one of those sea-captains about whom in the fifties we used to hear a great deal on the Devonshire coast' (*E*, p. 113).]

August? AT storms into a Post Office at Falmouth, Cornwall, booted and spurred, to carry out inspection. According to an official's recollections, he frightens almost out of his wits a rural messenger whose walk he was about to test. The man is so flustered that he puts a pound's worth of penny stamps into his hat and claps it on his head, where they stick fast. AT roars with laughter and invokes a barber's aid for the poor man.

At Penzance AT meets his match in the local postmistress, whose temper matches her tongue. After his usual peremptory introduction she orders him out. They afterwards become friends.

Inspecting rural posts in the far west of Cornwall, AT visits Mousehole, near Penzance. After some hostile exchanges he threatens to report the postmistress. She replies, 'Report me wusta? And I be'n so civil toee, too. Thees't better report my tuppence-farden a day.' [She becomes the model for Mrs Crump in *The Small House at Allington*.]

September During a stay in South Wales, Rose and the children enjoy sea air and bathing at Llanstephan. 'Harry and Freddy are quite well, and are very nice boys! – very different in disposition, but neither with anything that I could wish altered' (*L*, i, 31).

November AT arrives at a country post office saying, 'I have
walked up from Cardiff [some 24 miles]. Any hotels here; which
is the best?' Given directions he marches off at a six-mile-an-hour
stride saying, 'Back soon, going to have a raw beef steak.' The
postman from a nearby village asks for a pay increase, threatening
to resign. AT glowers, 'Look here, my man, don't think that we
cannot manage without you. Throw it up; there will be twenty
after your place to-morrow.'

24? November First roadside letter boxes open in Channel Islands,
with collections twice daily except Sunday. Within two weeks
requests come in from rural districts on the islands for their own
boxes. [By the mid-1850s pillar boxes were in use widely in
England.]

25 November AT applies unsuccessfully for the post of Superintendent of Mail Coaches. Sir John Trollope (1800–74) writes to
Lord Hardwicke, Postmaster-General, on AT's behalf pointing out
his twenty years' service: 'I have every reason to believe he is one
of your most able officers' (*L*, ɪ, 31).

1853

March TAT's daughter Beatrice, known as 'Bice' (d. 1881), is
born.

April AT and Rose visit his mother and TAT at the Villino
Trollope, Florence. Rose is again impressed by her mother-in-law's
energy. 'She took me about everywhere, and explained everything
to me. . . . The most charming old lady who ever existed' (*H*,
p. 254).

19 April–31 May On leave; goes abroad with Rose and John
Tilley, spending May in Florence with TAT.

29 July Begins work on *The Warden* at Tenbury, Herefordshire.
'It was then more than twelve months since I had stood for an
hour on the little bridge in Salisbury, and had made out to my
own satisfaction the spot on which Hiram's hospital should stand'
(*Auto.*, p. 83).

29 August　Moves to Belfast as acting Surveyor, Northern District of Ireland, with jurisdiction over Ulster and the counties of Meath and Louth.

5 September　Begins new duties in the Northern District of Ireland.

At the end of the year, Rose's father, Edward Heseltine, retires as manager of the Rotherham office of the Sheffield and Rotherham Joint Stock Company on health grounds. [Next year evidence comes to light that he had defrauded the company of between £4000 and £5000. He flees to France early in 1855 to avoid criminal proceedings.]

1854

31 January–4 February　Attends a meeting of surveyors in Glasgow to revise postal links between Ireland and Northern England.

15 June　Leaves Belfast to make his headquarters in Dublin.

28 June　Plans a five-week holiday visiting Paris, Geneva, Milan and Venice, but the visit has to be postponed to the following year.

10–12 July　Brief holiday in London.

1–5 August　Short leave in Scotland.

Autumn　Completes *The Warden* (originally, 'The Precentor'), sending manuscript to William Longman (1813–77), partner in the old established firm, on 8 October.

9 October　Appointed permanent Surveyor of the Northern District on the retirement of the incumbent. 'I trust my state of vassalage is over' (*L*, i, 36). The new job increases his basic salary from £150 to £240, soon boosted to £700 due to an all-round revision of pay scales. In addition he receives £1 for every day away from headquarters, £30 for office rent and travel expenses. R. S. Smyth, who serves under him, recalls that Trollope 'was held out to the juniors in the service as a terror and my early experience of him was not calculated to remove such an impression' (*I & R*, p. 59).

1855

January Begins *Barchester Towers*.

5 January Publication of *The Warden*. 'The novel-reading world did not go mad about *The Warden*; but I soon felt that it had not failed as the others had failed. . . . At the end of 1855 I received a cheque for £9 8s. 8d. which was the first money I had ever earned by literary work' (*Auto.*, p. 85). [Friendly treatments by periodicals, stressing the novel's strongly drawn characters, certainly augured well. Some faults were found in moral focus and burlesque elements, but generally comment followed the *Spectator's* 'keen observation of public affairs, a pungent closeness of style, and great cleverness in the author' (xxviii [6 Jan 1855] 27–8).]

February–March Writes *The New Zealander*, a polemical work in the manner of Carlyle.

2 April Longman's reader advises against publication of *The New Zealander*: 'If you had not told me that this work was by the author of *The Warden* I could not have believed it. . . . All the good points in the work have already been treated of by Mr Carlyle, of whose *Latter-Day Pamphlets* this work, *both in style and matter*, is a most feeble imitation' (*L*, I, 42). Trollope reworks text through May 1856 [published Oxford, 1972, ed. N. John Hall].

25 April Rowland Hill circulates a memorandum to surveyors defining their duties. AT challenges ambiguities of style in the memo. Hill replies, 'You must be aware, Mr Trollope, that a phrase is not always intended to bear a literal construction. For instance, when I write one of you gentlemen, I end my letter with the words "I am, Sir, your obedient servant", whereas you know I am nothing of the sort' (F. E. Baines, *Forty Years at the Post Office* [1895] I, 135).

3 May–13 June FT and TAT meet AT and Rose in Venice. They travel together through the Ampezzo Pass, whence the men detour through the mountains before rejoining the ladies at Innsbruck.

12 May Resumes *Barchester Towers*. Writing as he travels on Post Office duties, he makes a portable tablet and discovers he can work as well in a railway carriage as at his desk. From this time keeps a diary entering day by day the number of pages written, 'so that if at any time I have slipped into idleness for a day or two, the record of that idleness has been there, staring me in the face, and demanding of me increased labour, so that the deficiency might be supplied' (*Auto.*, p. 103).

Mid-June   Takes residence at 5 Seaview Terrace, Donnybrook, near Dublin. [He and his family will stay there until 1859.] His sons attend school near Chester.

26 June–2 August   In London on Post Office business.

17?–27 July   Testifies before a parliamentary committee looking into postal arrangements in Southern Ireland. A statement notes his 'great knowledge and efficiency as an Officer of the Department' (*S*, p. 30).

15 September   Death of Rose's father, Edward Heseltine, at Le Havre.

October   The *Dublin University Magazine* publishes his article on changes afoot in the Civil Service in which he attacks proposals for examinations. [The architects of reform, Sir Charles Trevelyan and Sir Stafford Northcote, are to feature in his novel *The Three Clerks* (1858).]

16? October   Deals with reorganisation of mail deliveries by carriages between Strabane, Sligo and Donegal.

1856

25–30 January   Absent on leave in London.

11–17 February   Ill, confined to bed.

12 May   Resumes *Barchester Towers*.

28 May–2 June   Leave of absence.

8 July   FT writes from the Villino Trollope that she has grown 'most woefully *lazy* and this symptom is both new and disagreeable to *me*. But the degree of activity of which I have been wont to boast, and on which I have so often been complimented might have been accounted in my very best days as positive *idleness* when compared to what you manifest. Tom and I agree in thinking that you exceed in this respect any individual that we have ever known or heard of – and I am proud of being your mother – as well for this reason as for sundry others' (*L*, i, 44).

5–8 August   In London, on Post Office business.

9 August–17 September   On leave; goes abroad with Rose and John Tilley.

9 November   Completes *Barchester Towers* (published by Longman, May 1857). [Its reception guaranteed AT's place among newer contemporary novelists. 'The former tale [*The Warden*] was good, but this is better' (*Examiner*, 16 May 1857, p. 308). In a four-column review H. F. Chorley (?) declared that 'Mr Trollope has a happier art of drawing sketches from life, and striking off pungent sayings hot and vivid upon the page, than of elaborating the actions of a novel', but AT was clearly emerging as a skilful writer (*Athenaeum*, 30 May 1857, pp. 689–90).]

8 December   Joseph Cauvin, reader for Longman, criticises *Barchester Towers* for vulgarity, viewing it as inferior to *The Warden* and weak in plot: 'It would be quite possible to compress the three volumes into one without much detriment to the whole' (*L*, i, 46).

20 December   AT refuses to make substantial cuts to the novel.

1857

15 February   Begins *The Three Clerks*.

18 April   Despatches from Trim, Co. Meath, a report on house-to-house letter delivery to the Secretary of the Dublin Post Office.
    Around this time, AT writes 'A History of the Post Office in Ireland'. His seven-page account, part of the Postmaster-General's

annual report, claims, 'In no part of the United Kingdom has more been done for the welfare of the people by the use of railways for carrying mails and by the penny postage system than in Ireland' (*S*, p. 34) [Shortly after Dublin Post Office moved to a new building in Queen's Square, AT took a firm hand in organising staff. AT taxes with negligence a subordinate who has inaccurately recorded the times postmen return from their deliveries. The official replies that he has no watch. A few days later AT leaves, having recommended a clock be installed.]

18 August Completes *The Three Clerks* (published by Richard Bentley, Nov 1857). [The *Saturday Review* greeted this advance in AT's literary career with the pronouncement that here was a novelist 'who must be conscious that he has a real reputation within his grasp'. With more care he might produce characters almost to 'rival that delicate and touching creation of Mr Thackeray's genius' (IV [5 Dec 1857] 517–18). Other reviews praised the broadening scope of subject and milieu.]

24 August Begins *The Struggles of Brown, Jones, and Robinson; by One of the Firm* (breaks off, 7 Sep).

5 September–17 October On leave; goes abroad with Rose, travelling through the Alps, visiting Milan, Verona and other towns before reaching Florence, where they spend three weeks with TAT and FT, who has given up writing [her last novel, *Fashionable Life in Paris and London*, was published in 1856]. While in Florence, TAT sketches out a plot for AT's next novel, *Doctor Thorne*. It is the only time 'I have had recourse to other sources than my own brains for the thread of a story' (*Auto.*, pp. 99–100). Makes acquaintance with the Brownings, who later read *The Three Clerks*; 'the best of his three clever novels', notes Elizabeth Barrett Browning. 'I was wrung to tears by the third volume. What a thoroughly man's book it is!' (*WIR*, II, 188).

17 October Arrives in London from Dublin. Delivers manuscript of *The Three Clerks* to Richard Bentley (1794–1871).

20 October Begins *Doctor Thorne*.

1858

January

Negotiations with Bentley break down. AT rushes round to Edward Chapman to offer him the book for £400. 'Looking at me as he might have done at a highway robber who had stopped him on Hounslow Heath, he said that he supposed he might as well do as I desired' (*Auto.*, p. 101).

30–1   (Sat–Sun) Meets TAT in Paris en route to Alexandria on Post Office business.

February

1   (Mon) Visits Chartres and admires the stained glass of the cathedral. He struggles to write five pages daily.

Taking ship at Marseilles early this month, he endures a rough voyage, writing his allotted number of pages each day between bouts of sea sickness.

10   Arrives at Alexandria where he undertakes two missions. The first is to check whether bags rather than metal boxes will be suitable for shipping mail through Egypt to India. He is anxious about bags causing friction on the camels' backs and being accessible to theft by drivers eager to rip them open with their knives. His second task, successfully completed, is to negotiate with Nubar Bey rail routes via Alexandria and Suez for mail to India and Australia.

16   In Cairo.

16, 23   Sends detailed progress reports to Rowland Hill calculating times at each stage of the mailing process by sea and land. In the course of his meticulous computations he clocks the speed of camels as three miles an hour.

17   Visits the Pyramids.

March

11   (Thurs) Writes to his colleague Edmund Yates from Alexandria that he is about to set out for Jerusalem. Yates, also on assignment to Egypt, is urged to hear the howling dervishes at Cairo at one on a Friday. [Yates (1831–94), minor novelist and editor, and AT were to fall out over a gossip item concerning Thackeray (1811–63). See under May 1860.]

13–23   Visits the Holy Land.

31 Completes *Doctor Thorne* (published by Chapman and Hall,
    May 1858). [By now AT was a mainstay of the circulating
    library. A review in the *Leader* hailed him as 'one of the
    extremely select few who shine out like a constellation among
    the unnumbered lesser luminaries of the "circulating" firma-
    ment' (29 May 1858, pp. 519–20). A more general review of
    over 8000 words by R. H. Hutton (?) in the *National Review*,
    VII (Oct 1858) 416–35, soon followed by an article by E. S.
    Dallas in *The Times*, 23 May 1859, p. 12, recognised AT's stature
    among Mudie's clientele: 'This majestic personage [Charles
    Edward Mudie, 1818–90], whom authors worship and whom
    readers court, knows that at the present moment one writer
    in England is paramount above all others, and his name is
    Trollope.']

April
1   (Tues) Begins *The Bertrams*, part of which takes place in the
    Holy Land.
4   Travels home via Malta, Gibraltar and Spain.
9–15 In Malta looks into management of the Post Office, finding
    the office over-staffed.
23–8 Holidays for six days in the south of Spain between visits
    to study the Gibraltar Post Office. [Short stories arising from
    his stay will appear in the first volume of *Tales of All Countries*
    (published by Chapman and Hall, Nov 1861).]

May
10 (Mon) Reaches London.
25–6 With Rose, takes a holiday at Ollerton, in Sherwood Forest,
    Nottinghamshire.

June
1   (Tues) On leave till the 10th.
16 Edward Chapman (1804–80), co-founder of Chapman and
    Hall, turns down AT's projected *Brown, Jones, and Robinson*:
    'there is a strong impression abroad that you are writing too
    rapidly for your permanent fame' (*L*, I, 74).
11–23 AT travels to Scotland to restructure postal services in
    Glasgow: 'I walked all over the city with the letter-carriers,
    going up to the top flats of the houses, as the men would
    have declared me incompetent to judge the extent of their

labours had I not trudged every step with them. . . . The men would grumble, and then I would think how it would be with them if they had to go home afterwards and write a love-scene' (*Auto.*, p. 110). [During July and August and until mid-September he returns often to Glasgow.]

November

3 (Wed) Arrives in London charged with special mission to the West Indies 'to cleanse the Augean stables of our Post Office system there' (*Auto.*, p. 110). Subsequently attends briefing on work to be done and is given permission to travel almost at will throughout the Caribbean.

6 At a general meeting in the Returned Letter Room at St Martin's le Grand, John Tilley launches the Post Office Library plan. AT speaks warmly in favour of the proposal. He begins by praising the Civil Service: 'I myself, love the Post Office. I have belonged to it ever since I left school. I work with all my heart, and everyone should do the same.' He hopes that the reading room will be provided with comfortable chairs: 'We can't be comfortable on a deal board, and without a good fire and a nice carpet' (*St Martin's le Grand*, xii [1902] 131–40). [See Appendix B.]

16 Leaves London 'in great force'.

17 Sails from Southampton on the steamship *Atrato*.

December

2 (Thurs) AT in St Thomas.

6 Arrives in Kingston aboard the *Derwent*.

25 Writes to a colleague, 'I am getting on with my work here, but it will I fear be very long before I get home. I am terribly bothered by the mosquitoes' (*L*, i, 79–80).

1859

The confidence St Martin's le Grand had in AT's administrative abilities now led to his most significant assignment, an extensive tour of the West Indies and Central America, which he discharged with exemplary thoroughness. The West Indies tour comprised

St Thomas (four times), Jamaica, Cuba, the Windward Islands, Barbados, St Vincent, Grenada, Trinidad, British Guiana, Santa Marta, Cartagena, Colón (twice), Costa Rica, Greytown (San Juan del Norte), Bermuda, New York, Niagara Falls, Liverpool. In Jamaica and British Guiana he had to investigate the transfer of postal arrangements to local agencies. In Cuba he was to negotiate treaties with the Spanish authorities; likewise in Panama with the government of New Granada, securing efficient, economical transfer of mails for routes to British Columbia, Australia and New Zealand.

En route to his first destination, 'he was able to propose a scheme of steamer routes more convenient and more economical than those in existence, "and, in the opinion of the hydrographer to the Admiralty, superior to them even in a nautical point of view" '. Jamaica he enjoyed, finding the country very lovely, although its chief town, Kingston, he thought unattractive. 'I went over the whole island, and saw as much of it, I flatter myself, as any man ever did in the time. I think I shall save the Post Office £1300 a year by my journey there. I like to feel that the expense has not been for nothing' (*L*, I, 81). At times the travelling was hard and rough. TAT recalls that, trying to prove in Central America that two days' ride could achieve what local officers reckoned could only be accomplished in three, AT stayed in the saddle so long the first day that when he arrived at his night stop he had to order two bottles of brandy. These he poured into a basin, sat in it, and thus recuperated for the next day's journey.

AT planned to meet up with Rose on the last leg of his journey in the United States, but this did not work out. He wrote as steadily as ever. His travel book *The West Indies and the Spanish Main* he came to regard 'as the best book that has come from my pen' (*Auto.*, p. 111), and several short stories emerged from the trip including, 'Miss Sarah Jack of Spanish Town, Jamaica' (*Tales of All Countries*, first vol.) and 'A Journey to Panama' (*Lotta Schmidt and Other Stories*).

Of his constant attention to official business (while finishing his novel *The Bertrams* in off-duty hours) R. H. Super notes that he doubtless spent time aboard ship learning about such 'technical matters as the effect of prevailing winds on the speed of vessels of different sizes, the condition of navigable passages between islands, and the location of suitable alternate harbours'. [For more information on this topic see *S*, pp. 38–44.]

January

3 (Mon) The Post Office Library and Literary Association opens its library and reading room to members, with 367 annual subscribers and over 2000 books. Early donors include the Prince Consort, the Duke of Argyll, H. G. Bohn, Harriet Martineau (1802–76) and Messrs W. H. Smith (some 300 volumes). The first donation is from Charles Dickens (1812–70), *Household Words* in 17 volumes. [William Henry Smith (1825–91), innovator of railway bookstalls, also had circulating-library interests rivalling Mudie's.]

17 Completes *The Bertrams* (published by Chapman and Hall, Mar 1859). [Power of characterisation and an entertaining tale are praised by reviewers, but warning notes about haste are sounded in the *Saturday Review*, vii (26 Mar 1859) 368–9, and the *Spectator*, xxxii (19 Mar 1859) 328–9: 'The fact is he writes too fast.']

24 Boards the brig *Linwood*, bound for the south coast of Cuba (arriving 2 Feb).

25 Starts *The West Indies and the Spanish Main* (finished in June and published by Chapman and Hall in October), which he writes while constantly on the move among the islands.

27 The *Linwood* makes slow progress, frequently becalmed, on what was to be a short cut to Cuba. 'I shall lose more time than I shall gain. I believe that in these days a man should never be tempted to leave the steam-boats' (*L*, I, 81).

April

9 (Sat) TAT agrees with Edward Chapman on his brother's behalf to the sum of £250 for three years for the travel book.

May

16 (Mon) Travels home via Bermuda and New York (9–12 June), making trips to Montreal (15–16 June) and Niagara Falls before boarding the Cunard ship *Africa*.

June

22 (Wed) Sails for England.

July

Possibly this month, writes two short stories later collected in the first volume of *Tales of All Countries*.

3 (Sun) Arrives in Liverpool.

(Mid-month) Appointed Surveyor of the Eastern District of England, his territory to include Essex, Suffolk, Norfolk, Cambridgeshire, Huntingdonshire, and eastern parts of Bedfordshire and Hertfordshire.

16   Reports to the Post Office with recommendations for revision of postal services in the Caribbean.

August

2   (Tues) Leases Waltham House, Waltham Cross, Hertfordshire, about 12 miles north-east of London. Frederic Chapman (1823–95), partner in the firm, agrees to pay £600 on publication of Trollope's next novel, *Castle Richmond* (published May 1860). [Irish novels being out of fashion, *Castle Richmond* was less widely reviewed than its predecessors.]

4   Begins *Castle Richmond*. During the month Post Office business takes him to Manchester, Liverpool, Dublin, Glasgow and Edinburgh.

September

7   (Wed) Goes on leave till 21 October; travels to Pyrenees with Rose, TAT and John Tilley; writes five short stories later collected in *Tales of All Countries*.

October

23   (Sun) Writes to Thackeray, suggesting he (AT) should contribute short stories for the new *Cornhill Magazine*. [George Smith had engaged Thackeray, who volunteered the name, to write the opening serial, and act as editor with Smith's assistance. Smith (1824–1901), head of Smith, Elder and Co., becomes one of AT's close friends.]

26   Smith welcomes AT to the *Cornhill* by inviting him to write a serial novel for the new magazine.

28   Thackeray writes warmly to AT, inviting further contributions to the periodical. 'Whatever a man knows about life and its doings that let us hear about. You must have tossed a deal about the world, and have countless sketches in your memory and your portfolio. . . . There was quite an excitement in my family one evening when Paterfamilias (who goes to sleep over a novel almost always when he tries it after dinner) came up stairs to the Drawing Room wide awake and calling for the second volume of *The Three Clerks* (*L*, I, 91).

November

Early this month, AT calls on Smith to offer his novel about Ireland for the *Cornhill Magazine*. Smith asks for a clerical tale and offers to double the largest sum AT had previously been offered for a novel (£500).

2 (Wed) Begins *Framley Parsonage*. 'This was the fourth novel of which I had placed the scene in Barsetshire, and as I wrote it I made a map of the dear county' (*Auto.*, p. 132).

21 Moves to Waltham Cross. Takes up duties as Surveyor for the Eastern District (appointment official on 10 Jan).

25 At Smith's request he cuts a page from *Framley Parsonage* 'but it was as tho you asked for my hearts [*sic*] blood' (*L*, I, 92).

December

Early this month, advises on reorganising postal establishments for Liverpool, Manchester and Birmingham. Travels during the month to Norwich, Yarmouth, Colchester.

1860

AT's fame as a novelist dates from his association with George Smith and the launching of *Framley Parsonage*, described below. He was so delighted with Thackeray's welcome to the new periodical that in due course he included the letter in his *Autobiography*. Connection with the *Cornhill*, moreover, went far to exorcise the loneliness of his childhood and early adult life. At Smith's table (he gave frequent *Cornhill* dinners) he could meet literary men on equal terms. His move to Waltham Cross similarly widened his social and sporting acquaintance, and then, by joining clubs, notably the Garrick and the Athenaeum, he found the approbation he had so desperately longed for. 'I have long been aware of a weakness in my own character', he was to write in later years, 'which I may call a craving for love. I have ever had a wish to be liked by those around me' (*Auto.*, p. 136). Among the club circle were Sir Charles Taylor, John Everett Millais, W. H. ('Billy') Russell of *The Times* and, of course, Thackeray, Charles Lever (known from the days in Ireland) and G. H. Lewes, whose friendship led Trollope to warm affection for George Eliot. So far as the Post Office went, his reputation was now so secure that he could ask for nine months leave in order to travel to North America (despite opposition from Rowland Hill), where once more new experiences added fuel to his literary furnace and brought him more friends literary and professional among the Boston Brahmins and legislators. Here also he befriended Kate Field (1838–96), the ardent girl he speaks of as 'out of my own family, my most chosen friend' (*Auto.*, p. 271). Another tribute besides Thackeray's he fondly quoted will be familiar to all Trollopians, the words of Nathaniel Hawthorne to James T. Fields in February 1860: 'Have you ever read the novels of Anthony Trollope? They precisely suit my taste, – solid and substantial, written on the strength of beef and through the inspiration of ale, and just as real as if some giant had hewn a great lump out of the earth and put it under a glass case, with all its inhabitants going about their daily business, and not suspecting that they were being made a show of' (*Auto.*, p. 125).

Probably at some time this year AT joins intermittently in meetings of artists at Arthur Lewis's chambers over a fruit shop in Jermyn Street. Here part-singing is provided by the Moray Minstrels. Leighton, Millais, Holman Hunt are among the regulars. [In 1864 Lewis founds the Arts Club in Hanover Square, which AT joined for some three or four years.]

January
Early this month, dines with George Smith in celebration of the *Cornhill* launch. Also present are Thackeray, Sir Charles Taylor, Field Marshal Sir John Burgoyne, R. Monckton Milnes, Frederick Leighton, J. E. Millais and Robert Browning. 'It was a memorable banquet in many ways, but chiefly so to me because on that occasion I first met many men who afterwards became my most intimate associates. It can rarely happen that one such occasion can be the first starting-point of so many friendships' (*Auto.*, p. 127). Things did not go quite so well. Eagerly anticipating meeting Thackeray he was rebuffed with a curt 'How do?' Later he called on Smith in wrathful mood. 'He vowed he would never speak to Thackeray again' (Leonard Huxley, *The House of Smith, Elder* [privately printed 1923] p. 104). G. A. Sala (1828–96) recalls that at the dinner AT was 'very much to the fore, contradicting everybody; afterwards saying kind things to everybody, and occasionally going to sleep on sofas or chairs; or leaning against side-boards, and even somnolent while standing erect on the hearthrug' (Sala, *Things I Have Seen and People I Have Known* [1894] i, 30–1).

Also this month, the first instalment of *Framley Parsonage* appears in the *Cornhill*. The magazine breaks records, selling 120,000 copies. AT's chance arose because Thackeray procrastinated over *Lovel the Widower*: 'My fitness lay in my capacity for quick roasting' (*Thackeray* [Macmillan, 1879] p. 52). [*Framley Parsonage* appeared in book form in April 1861, once serialisation had finished. The peak of AT's career so far, the novel was widely praised for its 'hearty feeling' (*Examiner*, 20 Apr 1861, pp. 244–5). The *London Review*, II (11 May 1861) 544–5, commented, 'Mr Trollope has now got his foot fairly in the stirrup' and emphasised 'health and manliness' as his prime virtues. The *Westminster Review*, LXXVI (July 1861) 282–4, grumbled at its triviality, while both the *Saturday Review*, XI (4 May 1861) 451–2, and the *Dublin University Magazine*, LIX (Apr 1862) 405–6, took a similar line on characters turning up again.]

10 Official appointment as Surveyor of the Eastern District. In the coming months AT visits Ipswich, Cambridge, Ely, Yarmouth and Norwich.

February

12 (Sun) In Cambridge. Writes to Smith, 'Should I live to see my story illustrated by Millais no body would be able to hold me' (*L*, I, 97). [John Everett Millais (1829–96) becomes Trollope's favourite illustrator and a close friend: 'To see him has always been a pleasure. His voice has been a sweet sound in my ears' (*Auto.*, p. 129).]

March

Millais illustrates *Framley Parsonage* from its third number.

2 Edward Fitzgerald (1809–83) writes to Stephen Spring Rice, 'I am awaiting another Box from Mudie: when some Novels of Trollope's will, I hope come. . . . Trollope's are very good, I think; not perfect, but better than a narrower Compass of Perfection like Miss Austen's' (*The Letters of Edward Fitzgerald*, ed. A. M. and A. B. Terhune [Princeton, NJ, 1980] II, 354).

April

2 (Mon) Joins a committee set up by John Tilley to examine charges (made in *The Times*, 29–30 Mar) that 'the Post Office regarded itself as a source of revenue, not as a service' (*S*, p. 48), and that lower grades were underpaid and exploited.

19 Elizabeth Barrett Browning (1806–61) expresses to Isa Blagden (1817–73) her delight in *Framley Parsonage* but finds fault with AT's grammar.

21 Committee resigns when its freedom of action appears threatened, but resignations not accepted by Hill.

24 Hill suspends committee, suspecting intrigue against himself, pending appointment of a new Postmaster-General.

26 AT and Tilley testify before parliamentary committee on Civil Service appointments. Questioned by Sir Stafford Northcote (1818–87), AT speaks out against examinations.

30 Tilley reinstates committee under certain restrictions; committee objects to restrictions and is subsequently reconstituted with two representatives of the Treasury and AT still a member.

May

1 (Tues) TAT comes for a two-week visit to Waltham House. Guests for dinner include a minor author, Sophia Coulton.

12 James T. Fields (1817–81), partner in the Boston publishing firm of Ticknor and Fields, visits AT and dines at Waltham House.

16 Deliberations begin of revised civil servants' appointments committee. It meets in 17 sessions over a period of six weeks.

19 Fields meets AT again at *Cornhill* dinner.

This month, AT relays a conversation with Thackeray and Smith at a Garrick Club dinner to Edmund Yates, who publishes it as a gossip item in 'Echoes from the London Clubs', *New York Times* (26 May). The *Saturday Review* takes it up (23 June) and Thackeray retaliates with a 'Roundabout Paper' for the *Cornhill*, 'On Screens in Dining-Rooms' (2 Aug). [This prolonged the Garrick Club Affair, which had set Dickens and Thackeray at odds.] AT confesses his role to Smith: 'I know I have done wrong and you may say anything you like to me' – [George Smith, 'Our Birth and Parentage', *Cornhill Magazine*, LXXXIII (Jan 1901) 4–17.]

Possibly this month, AT visits the Brownings. Elizabeth Barrett Browning notes in a letter, 'I like both brothers – the novelist is surpassingly clever as a writer – don't you think? And he has a very kind feeling for me, I understand from those who bear witness' (*Letters of the Brownings to George Barrett*, ed. Paul Landis [Urbana, Ill., 1958] p. 244).

20 Fields urges Hawthorne to come to London to meet Trollope. 'I told him you were a reader of his books and he seemed

really delighted that you praised his novels' (James C. Austin, *Fields of the 'Atlantic Monthly': Letters to an Editor, 1861–70* [San Marino, Calif., 1953] p. 212).

24 Thackeray writes to Mrs George Baxter, 'I think Trollope is much more popular with *Cornhill Magazine* readers than I am: and doubt whether I am not going down hill considerably in public favour' (*The Letters and Private Papers of W. M. Thackeray*, ed. Gordon N. Ray, [1946] IV, 236).

26 Meets the Leweses for the first time in Florence. [George Henry Lewes (1817–78) and George Eliot (1819–80) became close friends of AT.]

July

3 (Tues) Chapman and Hall agree to pay £2500 (£125 for each of 20 monthly parts) for *Orley Farm*, AT's first venture into shilling part issues (Mar 1861–Oct 1862).

4 Begins *Orley Farm*.

5 George Smith proposes a book on India, for which he is willing to pay £3000. AT is also to contribute two articles for the *Cornhill*. The project falls through.

9 AT seeks nomination for Charles Lee Lewes (son of GHL) for clerkship in the Post Office. Lewes notes in his journal (23 July), 'I only asked him for information, yet he most kindly interested himself and wrote to the Duke of Argyll' (*GE*, III, 326).

20 Advises GHL that his son will have to sit a competitive examination but is optimistic: 'I know no basis for a literary career, so good as an appointment in the C[ivil] Service – always presuming the man to be one who must live by the sweat of his brow' (*L*, I, 111).

21 Parliamentary committee completes and submits a 27-page report calling for improvements in salary scales for lower workers in Post Office service.

August

A contrite AT acknowledges his blunder over the Yates–Thackeray business and is reconciled with Thackeray.

4 (Sat) In Cambridge.

14 Advises GHL that his son has secured appointment in the Post Office.

September

24 (Mon) Rose and AT leave for Italy. Their journey includes
    stops at Naples, Florence (1–10 Oct) and Rome, returning
    home by 4 November.

October

Meets Kate Field in Florence: 'AT is a very delightful companion. I
see a great deal of him.' She asks him to obtain for her a copy of
the *Arabian Nights*. He promises to inscribe it and write a four-page
letter on condition that she writes back (Lilian Whiting, *Kate Field:
A Record* [Boston, Mass., 1899] p. 127). [Later she recalls the
brothers together: 'Thomas Trollope – looking half Socrates and
half Galileo – whom Mrs Browning called "Aristides the Just", and
the almost boyish enthusiasm and impulsive argumentation of
Anthony Trollope, who is an admirable specimen of a frank and
loyal Englishman' (*New York Tribune*, 22 Dec 1880).]

31 (Wed) Calls on the Brownings. Elizabeth Barrett Browning
    notes, 'Anthony has an extraordinary beard to be grown in
    England, but is very English in spite of it, simple, naif, direct,
    frank – everything one likes in a man – Anti-Napoleonist of
    course, and ignorant of political facts more than of course and
    not withstanding that, caring for *me* – which is strange, I
    admit' (*Letters of the Brownings*, ed. Landis, pp. 247–8).

November

 6 (Tues) Discusses serialisation of *Orley Farm* with George Smith
    and Frederic Chapman.

13 Mrs Fanny Stirling (1813–95), actress, wife of Sir Charles
    Hutton Gregory, consults AT about dramatising scenes from
    Framley Parsonage.

15 After Thackeray has rejected his short story 'Mrs General
    Talboys' as too strong for the *Cornhill*, AT replies, 'Pure morals
    must be supplied', but makes a strong statement on the
    writer's freedom to tackle subjects that only the squeamish
    and narrow-minded find offensive.

20 Dinner with the Leweses, described later by GE as 'a pleasant
    evening'; AT 'made us like him very much by his straightfor-
    ward, wholesome *Wesen*' (*GE*, IV, 360).

December

Early this month, changes to postal-delivery arrangements in areas
of Essex bring a complaint from the Rector of Lawford, near

Manningtree, who turns out to be Charles Merivale, fellow Harro-
vian of 35 years ago, and brother of AT's close friend John Merivale.

7 (Fri) Pointing out to Merivale that giving postal-delivery
   advantages to Lawford would provoke 20 complaints from
   East Bergholt, AT reminds his friend that at least he gets his
   letters before breakfast. 'I have just got back from Rome, where
   I learned that the Pope has but one delivery daily – his letters
   reaching the Vatican at 11 – all too early and all too often as
   he thinks. So at least it is whispered among the Cardinals'
   (*L*, I, 133). [Trollope enjoyed such exchanges and his travels
   about the eastern counties, drawing on place names such as
   Clavering, Ongar and Belton for his novels. For these and
   other details of his routine duties see *S*, pp. 45–8.]

15 From now until the turn of the new year AT organises
   his lecture panel for the Post Office Library and Literary
   Association. GHL is recruited to speak on 'Life from the Simple
   Cell to Man'. [Thackeray declines, but other participants
   include Edmund Yates ('Good Authors at a Discount', 18 Jan
   1861), Thomas Hughes ('The Printing Press', 1 Feb 1861),
   George Grossmith ('Lecturing', 1 Mar 1861), Thomas Hood
   Junior and John West.]

17 Attends with many literary men the opening of enlarged
   premises in New Oxford Street of Mudie's circulating library.
   [Charles Edward Mudie's library, founded in 1842, dominated
   Victorian reading habits for another quarter-century. E. S.
   Dallas (1828–79) commented in *The Times*, 23 May 1859, 'To be
   unknown to Mudie is to be unknown to fame.' Mudie was
   the Apollo of the circulating library and Trollope was his star:
   'He is at the top of the tree; he stands alone; there is nobody
   to be compared with him'.]

1861

January

4 (Thurs) AT delivers his lecture 'The Civil Service as a Profession', first of a series to raise money for the Post Office Library.
   The lecture is published in the February issue of *Cornhill*,
   which rouses Hill's wrath. He asks the Postmaster-General,
   Lord Stanley (1802–69), to censure AT, but Stanley declines,
   having seen the article in proof. [The lecture is included in
   Four Lectures, ed. Morris L. Parrish (privately printed, 1938).]

February

15 (Fri) GHL lectures at a meeting of the Post Office Library and Literary Association, and considers his contribution 'immensely successful'.

28 Parliamentary committee reconvened to reply to Hill, who had complained of Tilley's conduct in the affair.

March

Orley Farm begins appearing in monthly numbers, continuing until October 1862 (book publication: vol. I, Dec 1861; vol. II, Sep 1862). [After the disastrous serial publication of *The Struggles of Brown, Jones and Robinson*, critics rallied for *Orley Farm*, the *Saturday Review* pronouncing, 'No one has ever drawn English families better – without exaggeration, and without any attempt at false comedy' (XIV [11 Oct 1862], 444–5). A more incisive evaluation by R. H. Hutton (1826–97) declared, 'No English novelist has ever yet delineated the finer professional lines of English character with anything like his subtlety and power' (*Spectator*, XXXIII [11 Oct 1862] 1136–8). Reviews generally detected a more subtle analysis of human nature and social forces, a response typified by an unsigned essay, 'Orley Farm', in the *National Review*, XVI (Jan 1863) 27–40.]

7 (Thurs) Charles Merivale invites AT to dine next Monday, the 11th, and stay the night. Guests include the Revd Foster Barham Zincke (1817–93), writer of travel books.

11 Merivale writes to his mother, 'The P.O. is constantly blundering, notwithstanding the whitewashing it gets in *The Times*, and the numerous complaints I made myself to Trollope about it' (*L*, I, 132).

13 Hunting in Essex: 'We had a wretched day of it today – ploughing about thro the mud & rain – all day in the woods – our great success was the digging out of one fox' (*L*, I, 142). [From his earliest initiation into the sport AT was its passionate advocate, writing hunting scenes in his fiction wherever possible. As he later put it, 'The cause of my delight in the amusement I have never been able to analyse to my own satisfaction. . . . I ride still after the same fashion, with a boy's energy, determined to get ahead if it may possibly be done, hating the roads, despising young men who ride with them, and with a feeling that life can not, with all her riches, have given me anything better than when I have gone through a

long run to the finish, keeping a place, not of glory, but of credit, among my juniors' (*Auto.*, pp. 147–8).]

20 Signs an agreement with Chapman and Hall for a book on North America for £2000.

April

7 (Sun) Mrs S. C. Hall (1800–81) invites AT to join the staff of *St James's Magazine*. He declines, but contributes one article, 'The National Gallery' (Sep 1861).

8 AT is among nine surveyors asking the Postmaster-General for a revision of salary scales. [Another signatory is William Gay, who later recalled a visit from AT: 'No more repose was left in the house when he awoke in the morning. Doors slammed, footsteps resounded, and a general whirlwind arose, as he came or returned from his bath, or walked out in the garden, and from that time until nightfall, he was as busy as a man could be' (Susan E. Gay, *Old Falmouth* [1903] pp. 216–17). On another occasion AT amused his colleagues by interrupting the discussion with 'I differ from you entirely! What was it you said?' (*Edmund Yates: His Recollections and Experiences* [1884] I, 392).]

9 Rowland Hill forwards AT's leave application (to tour America) to the Postmaster-General, pointing out it is unprecedented and 'in many respects objectionable'. Lord Stanley responds that AT could be asked to help negotiate postal arrangements. Stanley grants the leave, which is a rebuff to Hill.

15 GHL dines and sleeps at Waltham. 'He [AT] has a charming house and grounds, and I like him very much, so wholesome and straightforward a man' (*GE*, IV, 426).

24 Richard Monckton Milnes (1809–85), later Lord Houghton, informs AT he has been elected to the Cosmopolitan Club [original for the 'Universe' in *Phineas Redux*].

May

5 (Thurs) Dinner at Thackeray's with Synge, the Folletts, the Collinses, Comyn, Craigie and Miss Russell.

15 Robert Bell (1800–67) enlists AT as steward for the annual dinner of the Royal Literary Fund. AT responds to the toast 'The Literature of England', becomes a life member of the Fund and ardent supporter of its aid to writers and their dependants. [He serves six times as steward for the dinners,

speaks on seven occasions, and from 1869 is one of three trea-
surers. See R. H. Super, 'Trollope at the Royal Literary Fund',
Nineteenth-Century Fiction, XXXVII, no. 3 (Dec 1982) 316–28.]

26 At the Cosmopolitan Club for a special gathering of members
and guests to greet the Duc d'Aumale (1822–97), elected
honorary member. Among those present are Matthew Higgins
(Jacob Omnium), Coningham (MP for Brighton), Hughes,
Stephen, Charles Bowen, Egerton, T. Bruce, Arthur Russell
(1825–92, the nephew of Lord John Russell), Chichester Fortescue, Lord de Grey and Dr George Henry Kingsley, the
travel writer (1827–92). [Chichester Fortescue, Lord Carlingford
(1823–98), Irish MP and landowner, was a possible model for
Phineas Finn.]

June
22 (Wed) Completes *Orley Farm*.
24 Resumes *The Struggles of Brown, Jones, and Robinson*.

July
2   (Sat) Meets George Smith.
4   Dinner with GE and GHL followed by a meeting with the
Carlyles at Cheyne Walk. In a letter to TAT, GHL recalled the
day: 'Yesterday Anthony dined with us, and, as he had never
seen Carlyle, he was glad to go down with us to tea at Chelsea.
Carlyle had read and *agreed* with the West Indian book, and
the two got on very well together; both Carlyle and Mrs Carlyle
liking Anthony – and I suppose it was reciprocal, though I
did not see him afterwards to hear what he thought. He had
to run away to catch his train' (*GE*, VIII, 287). [Carlyle (1795–
1881), social prophet and critic, was later angered by AT. See
entry for 15 July 1865.]

August
1   (Mon) *Brown, Jones, and Robinson* begins serialisation in the
Cornhill (continued until Mar 1862; book publication by Smith,
Elder, Nov 1870). [The tone of criticism was set by the
Westminster Review, which declared that 'the whole affair was
a blunder' (xcv [July 1871] 574–5).]

3   Completes *Brown, Jones, and Robinson*. [Reviews are distinctly
unfavourable. The *Illustrated London News* (10 Aug) declares,
'nobody can understand what Mr Trollope means'.]

5   AT is invited to take on 'ostensible' editorship of *Temple Bar* if
he will supply a novel. The invitation states, 'All the real work

of editorship will be performed – as heretofore – by Mr Edmund Yates, who would act with you as sub-editor.' Aghast, AT declines, noting, 'would not undertake a mock-editorship' (*L*, I, 157).

24 Leaves from Liverpool with Rose for the United States. Arriving in Boston, they prepare to make a circuit through Canada to Detroit and back east along the American side of the Great Lakes.

AT's American itinerary: (with Rose) Boston, Newport, Portland, White Mountains, Quebec, Montreal, Ottawa, Toronto, Niagara, Windsor, Detroit, Grand Haven, Milwaukee, St Paul, Minneapolis, Dubuque, Chicago, Cleveland, Buffalo, Utica, Trenton Falls, Albany, West Point, Boston (Rose returns to England on 27 Nov); (alone) Baltimore, Harrisburg, Altoona, Pittsburgh, Cincinnati, Lexington, Frankfort, Louisville, St Louis, Rolla, St Louis, Cairo, Louisville, Camp Wood, Seymour, Cincinnati, Crossline, Pittsburgh, Altoona, Harrisburg, Baltimore.

September

5 (Mon) Arrives at Boston.

6 Dines with Charles Sumner (1811–74, leading Massachusetts senator) and Dr Samuel Kirkland Lothrop (1804–86, minister of Brattle Square Unitarian Church) at Lothrop's home.

13 Meets Mary Knower (1840?–1931) at Newport.

16 Begins *North America*. Meets Nathaniel Hawthorne when he dines at J. T. Fields' with J. R. Lowell (1819–91), O. W. Holmes (1809–94) and Emerson (1803–82). Holmes, 'The Autocrat', engages in verbal battles with AT to everyone's amusement, while Emerson and Lowell crouch down 'out of range, with the shot hurtling overhead'. In a letter to Hawthorne, Fields wrote, 'Trollope fell in love with you at first sight and went off moaning that he could not see you again. He swears you are the handsomest Yankee that ever walked this planet' (Austin, *Fields of the 'Atlantic Monthly'*, p. 215). Lowell describes AT as 'a big, red-faced, rather underbred Englishman of the bald with spectacles type. A good roaring positive fellow who deafened me (sitting on his right) till I thought of Dante's Cerberus' (H. S. Scudder, *James Russell Lowell: A Biography* [1901] II, 82).

(Mid-month) Meets the opera singer Clara Louise Kellogg, Mme Strakosch (1842–1916), at the Fieldses'. 'Trollope was full of himself and wrote only for what he could get out of it', comments the prima donna. 'I never, before or since, met a literary person who was so frankly "on the make"' (Clara Louise Kellogg, *Memoirs of an American Prima Donna* [New York, 1913] p. 48).

23   Visits Quebec.
30   Visits Montreal and continues to Ottawa (3 Oct) and Toronto (5–7 Oct).

October
 8–9   (Tues–Wed) At Niagara Falls. Much of the month is devoted to exploring in Buffalo, Detroit, Milwaukee, Chicago and other cities, returning to New York on the 30th.

November
Early this month, in New York for 10 days before travelling to Boston. Perhaps in this period meets Henry Theodore Tuckerman (1813–71), poet, essayist and critic. His brother, Charles K. Tuckerman (1821–96) described AT as 'a stout, hairy-faced, ruddy-complexioned Englishman . . . like a rough, shaggy Newfoundland dog. . . . In physique, manner, and speech he might have been taken for a dragoon in mufti, or a sportsman fresh from an invigorating run in the fields (*Personal Recollections of Notable People at Home and Abroad* [1895] ii, 8).
 3   (Sun) AT asks Fields to look after 32 volumes of James Fennimore Cooper's novels at his Boston home until he arrives about the middle of the month (he plans to stay there two weeks).
 5   Kate Field is taken to task for not being in New York: 'I have been real angry with you this week for not turning up' (*L*, i, 161).
 9   Attends address to the New York Historical Society by the historian George Bancroft (1800–1901). At one point he whispers to his companion, 'Do you suppose he himself believes what he is saying?'
22   Hears Edward Everett (1794–1864), statesman and editor of the *North American Review*, deliver his popular speech 'The Causes and Conduct of the Civil War' at Roxbury, Massachusetts. He comments later, 'I did not like what he said, or the seeming spirit in which it was framed. But I am bound to admit that his power of oratory is very wonderful' (*L*, i, 164).
25   ? The Trollopes dine with William Sturgis (1782–1863), former Massachusetts state legislator.

27 Rose returns to England. 'She has a house, and children & cows and dogs & pigs – and all the stern necessities of an English home', argues AT (*L*, I, 161).

28 Goes to Concord, Massachusetts.

29 Longfellow (1807–82) notes in his journal that Trollope called with Charles Eliot Norton (1827–1908), Professor of Arts at Harvard, and Lowell.

30 ? Dines with Emerson at his club.

December

24–31 (Tues–Tues) In Washington, dines several times with a Mr Russell. Some time during his stay in Washington, which continues until 12 January 1862, he meets Salmon P. Chase (1808–73), then Secretary of the Treasury.

27 Fanny Seward, 17-year-old daughter of William Henry Seward (1801–72), US Secretary of State, 1861–70, notes meeting AT, 'a great homely, red, stupid faced Englishman, with a disgusting beard of iron grey' (*L*, I, 165).

1862

January

1 (Wed) From Washington AT responds to Frederic Chapman about a hostile article in the *Literary Budget* (1 Dec 1861) accusing him of writing for money: 'Of course I do. . . . It is for money that we all work, lawyers, publishers, authors and the rest of us' (*L*, I, 167).

9 Breakfasts with R. H. Dana (1815–82) and others. Dana finds Trollope 'intolerable, no manners but means well, & would do a good deal to serve you, but says the most offensive things – not a gentleman' (*L*, I, 170).

12 Leaves Washington for Cincinnati.

14 GE writes of *Orley Farm* to Sara Sophia Hennell, 'Anthony Trollope is admirable in the presentation of even, average life and character, and he is so thoroughly wholesome-minded that one delights in seeing his books lie about to be read' (*GE*, VIII, 302).

20 From Cincinnati sends a farewell to Fields.

23–4 At Louisville, Kentucky.

25–8, 31 (also 1–2 Feb) At St Louis, Missouri.

February

3–5   (Mon) At Cairo, Illinois. 'Till I came here I thought St Louis
the dirtiest place in the world; but this place certainly bears
the palm' (*L*, I, 174).

March

3 or 4   (Mon or Tues) Meets Longfellow after his return from the
West.

8   ? Dines with William Sturgis.

10   Meets Mrs Harriet Knower.

12   Leaves New York for England, arriving at Liverpool on 25
March.

Late this month or early in April, Dr Norman Macleod (1812–72),
chaplain to Queen Victoria and editor of *Good Words*, 1860–72,
invites AT to write a story for the magazine: 'I think you could let
out the *best* side of your soul in *Good Words* – better far than even
in *Cornhill*' (*L*, I, 178).

April

5   (Sat) Elected to Garrick Club and becomes addicted to whist
in the afternoons. Robert Bell proposes and Thackeray seconds
his nomination.

7   Meets Alexander Strahan (1833–1918), publisher of *Good Words*,
Argosy and *Contemporary Review*, and agrees to supply a one-
volume novel. [On 5 Dec arranges to double the length. The
book, *Rachel Ray*, causes Macleod alarm. See p. 51.]

27?   Completes *North America* (published by Chapman and Hall,
May 1862).

May

1   (Thurs) Discusses with George Smith changing the name of
his proposed new novel from 'Two Pearls of Allington' to *The
Small House at Allington*.

11   Dines with Thackeray at the Star and Garter, Richmond.
Shortly before the 13th, Thackeray writes to William Webb
Follett Synge (1826–91), 'I have just met a Trojan of the name
of Trollope in the street (your ingenious note of last night kept
me awake all night, be hanged to you), and the upshot is that
we will do what you want between us'. [The circumstance
alluded to is a loan of £900 both Trollope and Thackeray made

when Synge was in dire need. AT, telling the story in his *Thackeray* (p. 60), omitted his own generous gesture.]

15 GHL is informed that his son is not doing well at the Post Office and has been sent back to the missing-letter branch. AT writes kindly, but candidly, that reports suggest he is careless, slow and idle (*L*, I, 181). [Possibly this brought back many memories of his own beginnings in the Service.]

20 Begins *The Small House at Allington*.

23 At Wisbech.

June

2 (Mon) GHL writes to TAT (*GE*, IV, 59) that he has read the first volume of *North America* 'and am immensely pleased with it – so much so, that I hope to do something towards counteracting the nasty notice in the *Saturday* [*Review*, XIII (31 May 1862) 625–6]', which described it as 'as thin-spun, tedious, mooning a journal of travel as has been offered to the public for a long time' GHL's comment appeared in the *Cornhill*, VI (1 July 1862) 105–7.

At the same time, TAT is visiting Waltham. AT sets up a dinner party for him and old friends, Mrs Mary Christie (1847–1906) and her brother Owen Grant, for 7 June.

11 Attends Alpine Club dinner at the Castle, Richmond, with Sir William Hardman (1828–90), William Longman and others. 'Anthony Trollope is also a good fellow, modelled on Silenus, with a large, black beard. There was a call for Trollope, and Silenus made a funny speech, assuring the Club that he was most desirous of becoming a member, but the qualification was the difficulty, and both time and flesh were against him' (*A Mid-Victorian Pepys: The Letters and Memoirs of Sir William Hardman*, ed. S. M. Ellis [1923] p. 143).

28 Congratulating GE on the first number of *Romola*, AT counsels her, 'Do not fire too much over the heads of your readers. You have to write to tens of thousands, & not to single thousands' (*L*, I, 187).

30 Visits the Revd S. W. King (1821–68), Rector of Saxlingham Nethergate, Norfolk.

July

5 (Sat) Dines with the gentlemen of the Old Bailey Printing Establishment (Smith, Elder and Co., printing office).

16   Longfellow acknowledges arrival of *North America*: 'I am sure
     to find it frank, outspoken, and friendly; and you are sure, in
     return, to find in me a friendly reader, and not a captious
     critic' (*L*, I, 188).
24   In Glasgow.

August
 3   (Sun) At Diss, Norfolk; for the rest of the month on the move
     in the eastern counties. For several weeks AT is troubled by
     Isa Blagden's problems in getting her novel *The Cost of a Secret*
     published. Chapman and Hall bring it out on the 23rd.
23   Kate Field having taken him to task for not giving her *North
     America*, he responds, 'One gives presentation copies to old
     fogies & such like. When you write a book, you will of course
     give one to me. You are a young lady – A ring, a lock of my
     hair, or a rosebud would be the proper present for you; not
     two huge volumes weighing no end of pounds' (*L*, I, 192).

September
 1   (Mon) *The Small House at Allington* begins serialisation in
     Cornhill (continued until Apr 1864; book publication by Smith,
     Elder, Mar 1864). [Readers and reviewers took kindly to the
     newest Barsetshire romance, dwelling on the unhappy triangle
     between Lily Dale, Johnny Eames and Adolphus Crosbie. For
     AT's grasp of subtleties in relationships the *Spectator* turned
     this memorable phrase: 'It is his command of what we may
     call the moral "hooks and eyes" of life that Mr Trollope's
     greatest power lies' (XXXVII, [9 Apr 1864] 421–3). The jilting of
     Lily Dale provoked some coy sallies, such as the note in the
     Illustrated London News, XLIV (16 Apr 1864) 375, that 'flesh and
     blood cannot endure that she should be sentenced to lead the
     life of a "widowed maid"'.
 6   The *Athenaeum* publishes AT's open letter on international
     copyright and literary piracy addressed to James Russell Lowell
     in which he refers to 'men, who, like us, earn our bread by
     writing'. The phrase angers Rowland Hill, who notes in his
     diary, 'Trollope is suspected of neglecting his duties official to
     attend to his literary labours – Engagement in connection with
     the *Cornhill Magazine* and another periodical whose name I do
     not recollect – numerous novels – Trip to the United States
     (1861–2) and work thereon' (*S*, p. 59).

13–23 On leave; goes to Holland.
16 Hill adds to his diary his opinion that AT is less than sincere and honest.
19 Browning writes to Isa Blagden of his regard for both Trollope brothers: 'I will not lose A. Trollope's company by any fault of my own for the Future' (*Dearest Isa: Robert Browning's Letters to Isabella Blagden*, ed. Edward C. McAleer [Austin, Texas, 1951] p. 124). [The poet (1812–89) was to become one of AT's close friends.]

October
18 (Sat) The *Athenaeum* prints AT's rejoinder to Fletcher Harper's letter on the international copyright issue.

November
This month and next, hunting in Oxfordshire as often as he can spare the time ('the fact is I have become a slave to hunting'). House guests at Waltham – 'all more or less in the boots & breeches line' – are amused until Christmas (*L*, I, 206).
21 (Fri) Returning from hunting, he buckles to writing a short story, 'The Widow's Mite', for *Good Words*.
24–30 Leave of absence from the Post Office.

December
8 (Mon) Delivers manuscript of his story to Alexander Strahan.
15 GE comments to Charles Bray on the effects of the Banting diet: 'Mr A. Trollope is thinner by means of it, and is otherwise the better for the self-denial' (*GE*, IV, 392).
30 AT delivers his lecture 'The Present Condition of the Northern States of the American Union', in the Midlands (?).

1863

January
13 (Tues) Delivers his lecture on the Northern states in London [text published in *Four Lectures*].
19 Browning writes to Isa Blagden that he is to dine with AT and GE next Thursday, the 22nd. He passes on some gossip concerning the paternity of Beatrice ('Bice') Trollope, daughter of Theodosia and TAT.

February
Tales of All Countries: Second Series (a collection of stories published
in periodicals during 1861) published by Chapman and Hall.
4   (Wed) Thackeray records in his diary visits from Rose Trollope,
    Archdeacon Sinclair, Kerrick Junior (Fitzgerald's nephew),
    Nassau Senior, Herman Merivale and others.
11 AT completes *The Small House at Allington*. Confined to bed
    with liver trouble and spends 10 days recuperating.
24 In response to request from Emily Faithfull (1836–95), feminist
    lecturer and publisher, sends short story, 'Miss Ophelia
    Gledd', for her book *A Welcome* (1863). ['The Journey to
    Panama' had appeared in her volume *Victoria Regia* (1861).]

March
Florence Nightingale Bland (b. 1855) becomes a member of the
Trollope household. [She is the orphaned daughter of Joseph Bland
and of Rose Trollope's sister, Isabella. AT became very fond of his
niece, who in later years acted as his amanuensis.]
3   (Tues) Begins *Rachel Ray*.

April
13 (Mon) Attacking literary fare offered by *Good Words*, another
    evangelical journal, the *Record*, labels AT 'the year's chief
    sensation writer' and (a week later) 'a secular novelist'.

May
10 (Sun) The Trollopes dine with Thackeray, O.(?) Gordon, the
    Charles Bagot Cayleys and the James Fitzjames Stephens.
    [Stephen (1829–94), later Sir James, renowned judge, was a
    prominent contributor to the *Pall Mall Gazette* and *Cornhill
    Magazine*.] AT invites M. J. O'Connell (1811–75), MP for County
    Kerry, for 18–20 May: 'There will be some people with us –
    but the eating will be poor. Our cook has got drunk, –
    perpetually drunk. If there be nothing to eat we can do the
    same' (*L*, I, 215).
12 AT learns he is to speak the next day at the anniversary dinner
    of the Royal Literary Fund at Willis's Rooms, St James's, in
    response to the toast 'The Writers of Fiction' proposed by
    Charles Merivale.
13 Merivale's speech at the Royal Literary Fund dinner praises
    'one from the keenness of whose analysis of human nature we

have all smarted, statesmen, bishops, lawyers, and country parsons, members of parliament, and newspaper editors, but again by whose genial humanity we have all been comforted and reassured'. In reply AT claims, 'Novel Writers of the country are the great instructors of the country. They help the church and they are better than the law. They teach ladies to be women, and they teach men to be gentlemen' (Super, *Nineteenth-Century Fiction*, xxxvii, 319–20).

20   Plans a dinner party but several guests default in favour of the Derby. AT goes to the Cosmopolitan for the evening. To Millais he writes next day, 'We had a very melancholy day – which wd have been less melancholy had you all come. But it could not be helped. My wife was awfully disgusted as women always are when nobody comes to eat their pastries and sweetmeats. As for me I hope you lost your money at the Derby' (*L*, i, 215).

June

11   (Thurs) The Revd Norman Macleod rejects *Rachel Ray* as inappropriate for readers of *Good Words*. AT comments, 'a letter more full of wailing and repentance no man ever wrote' (*Auto.*, p. 161). He demands and gets compensation of £500 from the publisher, Alexander Strahan.

12   W. H. Russell, Jacques Blumenthal, Emily Faithfull and Robert Bell invited to Waltham. [William Howard ('Billy') Russell (1820–1907), later Sir William, and Blumenthal (1829–1908), a composer, were fellow Garrick members.]

29   Completes *Rachel Ray* (published by Chapman and Hall, Oct 1863). [Generally regarded as lighter fare than its predecessor, *Rachel Ray* was praised for its light humour and understanding of the female psyche. The *Athenaeum* called it 'a portfolio of women's portraits, the like of which no artist but Mr Trollope could produce' (17 Oct 1864, pp. 492–4). The *Saturday Review* found it 'thin and slight' but never dull: 'it is his mission to keep on writing for ever about the inner life of girls, and the clergy, and vulgar families, and he always does it well' (xvi [24 Oct 1864] 554–5).]

July

Early this month, receives presentation copy of *Romola* from GE.

19   (Sun) AT runs into Browning at the Cosmopolitan Club, tells

him of his brother's arrival in London and tries to set up a
meeting.

20   Goes on leave till 15 August, taking a summer tour in the Alps
     with Rose, Henry and Fred.

August

16   (Sun) Begins *Can You Forgive Her?*, drawing on material from
     his rejected play, *The Noble Jilt*. [First full presentation of
     Plantagenet Palliser and Lady Glencora: 'They have served me
     as safety-valves by which to deliver my soul' (*Auto.*, p. 155).]

September

Early this month, Chapman and Hall plan a new periodical,
tentatively called the 'New Weekly', with AT as editor, but the
idea falls through.

 7   (Mon)? Meeting with Frederic Chapman.

10   Takes Harry, who has now left school, to Florence; returns on
     28 September. Work on his parliamentary series of novels,
     just begun, enables him to have 'that fling at the political
     doings of the day which every man likes to take, if not in one
     fashion then in another' (*Auto.*, pp. 155, 159).

28? Discusses publication of *Can You Forgive Her?* with Chapman.

October

 6   (Tues) Death of Frances Trollope. [Her last letter, undated but
     written seven years earlier, reads, 'My darling Anthony: You
     ask me to write – I and my pen have been so long divorced
     that I hardly know how to set about it – But you ask me to
     write and therefore write I will – though I have no news to
     tell you more fresh than that I love you dearly – I should like
     to see you again but can hardly hope it! God bless you my
     dear, dear Son! Your loving mother' (*H*, p. 255).]

23   Acknowledging a gift of *Rachel Ray*, GE describes it as 'a strictly
     related well proportioned whole, natty & complete as a nut
     on its stem. . . . But there is something else I care yet more
     about, which has impressed me very happily in all those
     writings of yours that I know – it is that people are breathing
     good bracing air in reading them – it is that they, the books
     are filled with belief in goodness without the slightest tinge of
     maudlin. They are like pleasant public gardens, where people

go for amusement, & whether they think of it or not, get
health as well' (*L*, ɪ, 238).

November

10 (Tues) Invites William Wilkins Glenn (1824–76), American
    journalist, for a hunting weekend: 'Perhaps you might like to
    see so thoroughly British an institution as a fox hunt' (*L*, ɪ, 241).
    [Glenn evidently appreciated the foxhounds, as he was invited
    again for Christmas Day.]

24 Attends the Leweses' housewarming and coming-of-age party
    for Charles Lewes at the Priory, Regent's Park, where GHL
    and GE had moved on the 5th. Among the guests are Henry
    Buxton Forman, John Payne, E. S. Dallas, the explorer and
    anthropologist R. F. Burton (1821–90), and the journalist
    E. F. S. Piggott (1824–95).

December

25 (Fri) Death of Thackeray. AT writes to George Smith, 'I felt it
    as a very heavy blow', and to Frederic Chapman, 'It has not
    been a merry Christmas with us. I loved him dearly' (*L*, ɪ, 244,
    245). 'I regard him as one of the most tender-hearted human
    beings I ever knew. . . . When he went from us he left behind
    living novelists with great names; but I think that they who
    best understood the matter felt that the greatest master of
    fiction of this age had gone' (*Auto.*, pp. 159, 160). [He contrib-
    utes an appreciation in *Cornhill*, ɪx (Feb 1864) 134–7.]

30 Attends Thackeray's funeral at All Souls' cemetery, Kensal
    Green. Some 1500 people present.

1864

January

1 (Fri) *Can You Forgive Her?* begins appearing in monthly numbers (published by Chapman and Hall, continuing until Aug
   1865; book publication in 2 vols, Sep 1864 and July 1865).
   [Strong characterisation in the figures of George Vavasor,
   Burgo Fitzgerald and Lady Glencora Palliser was the frequent
   theme of reviewers, the *Spectator* clearly seeing a new and
   major resource in the Pallisers: 'it is *her* [Lady Glencora's]

fortunes rather than Alice's that we watch with the most interest' (xxxviii [2 Sep 1865] 978–9).]

10   Millais visits Waltham House.

11   AT extends an invitation to John Leech (1817–64), Punch's chief cartoonist from early days, writer of sporting sketches, to join Millais and himself hunting the following Wednesday (the 13th).

26   At Bury St Edmunds to deliver his lecture 'Politics as a Daily Study for Common People'. 'I went there in a carriage with a marquis, who talked to me all the way about the state of his stomach which was very grand; and the room was quite full, and the people applauded with thorough good nature, only they did so in the wrong places' (L, i, 250). Next morning leaves at 6 a.m. to hunt 30 miles away.

28   Stays overnight with the Revd Charles Burney, Vicar of Halstead.

February
Possibly this month, attends performance of H. J. Byron's burlesque *Orpheus and Eurydice*.

4   (Thurs) Dines with the Leweses.

18   Attends meeting of Leeds Mechanics' Institution and Literary Society and repeats his lecture 'Politics as a Daily Study for Common People'.

25   Lectures at Halstead Literary and Mechanics' Institution on the American Civil War to a 'large and influential' audience.

March
2   (Wed) On hearing of Sir Rowland Hill's resignation, AT writes to express his admiration for his work: 'I have regarded you for many years as one of the essential benefactors, not only of your own country, but of all the civilized world' (L, i, 256). In his journal Hill in astonished tone wrote, 'Among the numerous letters of congratulation are . . . some even from men whom I have had too much reason to believe unfriendly. There is an excellent letter, among others, from Trollope' (S, p. 55).

9   Becomes a member of the General Committee of the Royal Literary Fund, which adjudicates on cases of hardship among writers and their dependants.

17 On the promotion of John Tilley as Secretary of the Post Office (after Rowland Hill's resignation), Frank Ives Scudamore (1823–84) gets Tilley's post as Assistant Secretary over AT's head. Scudamore is six years AT's junior in service and from the Receiver and Accountant-General's Office. The appointment causes strained relations between AT and his brother-in-law for a while.

21 Reports to GHL on having seen Carlyle the previous week: 'Oh heavens; – what a mixture of wisdom and folly flows from him!' (*L*, ɪ, 258).

April

4 (Mon) Isa Blagden informs Kate Field, 'I saw AT last autumn. He desired me to give his love to you and to say to you that he was always & ever your friend. He told me many things which surprised me, One that he had received wedding cards purporting to be from you [AT had passed a rumour that Kate Field had got married]' (McAleer, *Dearest Isa*, pp. 174, 188).

8 The Post Office surveyors join forces to make a case to the Postmaster-General, Lord Stanley, for salary-scale revision. The memorandum (in AT's hand) is addressed to John Tilley, who on the 21st rejects it on behalf of Stanley. AT responds warmly (8 July), objecting to a response 'so calculated to give offence'. He continues, 'I am a public servant of 30 years standing, and have never before either separately or jointly with others, requested a reconsideration of my Salary.' With a hint of his own career disappointment he adds, 'I also think that I am justified in asking his Lordship to recommend the newly appointed Secretary to be more considerate of the feelings of those Officers among whom he passed his official life, till he received his promotion.' Tilley, obviously stung, passes 'this most intemperate letter' to Stanley. From a holiday retreat at Windermere AT scores a last bull, writing to Stanley direct (18 July) in the knowledge that Tilley will see the letter. The merits of the case, he comments, had not been appreciated: 'It was exactly the way in which Oliver was treated when he came forward on behalf of the Charity boys to ask for more; – and I own that I thought Mr Tilley was very like Bumble in the style of the answer he gave us.' AT had lost the battle but his final salvo enabled him to leave the field with pride intact. [A fragment of a letter to an unknown correspondent on 27

July perhaps refers to the affair: 'My feeling is that a man should fight to the last if he feels himself to be right' (*L*, i, 272–8, 281).]

12   Elected to the Athenaeum Club under Rule ii (by special invitation) with the assistance of Lord Stanhope (1805–75).

16   Present at the Anniversary Festival of the Artists' General Benevolent Association in Freemasons' Hall, the Bishop of Oxford in the chair.

28   Completes *Can You Forgive Her?*

May

6   (Fri) Dines with Lord Houghton.

11   Attends meeting for the establishment of the Shakespeare Foundation Schools in connection with the Royal Dramatic College held at the New Adelphi Theatre. Dickens in the chair introduces supporting speakers, including AT. Edmund Yates moves a vote of thanks.

18   Royal Literary Fund anniversary dinner at St James's Hall, the Prince of Wales in the chair. AT responds to the toast 'Prosperity to English Literature, and the health of Mr Anthony Trollope', proposed by Earl Russell (1792–1878). AT eulogises Thackeray: 'He is one whom we all loved with an especial love, because no man's hand was ever open more often than his, and no man's hand was ever opened wider. . . . I do not think that we yet know how great that man was – I do not think that we have felt how deep was his pathos, how soft he was in his tenderness, how true he was in his delineations of character, how gracious he was in his conduct (*Cheers*)' (Bradford Booth, 'Trollope and the Royal Literary Fund', *Nineteenth-Century Fiction*, vii [1952] 212).

22   Begins *Miss Mackenzie*.

June

13   (Mon) Dinner at the Star and Garter, Richmond.

July

1   (Fri) A house party prevents AT from meeting Mrs Gaskell, then visiting the Smiths. Mrs Gaskell (1810–65) had greatly admired *Framley Parsonage*. [They never met before her death in November.] At this time AT's portrait is being painted by Samuel Laurence (1812–84) at George Smith's behest.

6   Dinner at the Garrick Club in its new home in Garrick Street.

As Chairman of the Committee, AT proposes a toast to Thackeray's memory.

13 Goes on leave with Rose in the Lake District (till 2 Aug).

August

18 (Thurs) Completes *Miss Mackenzie* (published by Chapman and Hall, Feb 1865). [By and large critical response turned on the skill through which such dull prosaic material was made lively and interesting. The *London Review* saw it as evidence of AT's skill that he should tackle seemingly unrewarding subject matter: 'but Mr Trollope revels in risk, and delights in surrounding himself with difficulties and dangers for the sake of the pleasure he finds in ultimately overcoming them' (x [8 Apr 1865] 387). Henry James (1843–1916), then at the start of his career, reviewed the novel tartly for the *Nation*, calling AT an exponent of 'quiet novels' preoccupied with mundane observations of ordinary levels of existence: 'His manner, like most of the literary manners of the day, is a small manner' (i [13 July 1865] 51–2).]

24 Begins *The Claverings*.

October

3 (Mon) Goes on leave till the 12th – to Paris with Harry, then to the Isle of Wight with Rose.

8 Crosses to Yarmouth, Isle of Wight, by steamer, accompanied by Rose. On the coach to Freshwater asks many practical questions about the houses and countryside – does not seem interested in Tennyson (1809–92).

10 Writes from Freshwater thanking George Smith for his portrait: 'I find myself to be a wonderfully solid old fellow' (*L*, i, 285). [One version of the picture is in the National Portrait Gallery.]

11 Accompanies (William) Frederick Pollock (1815–88) to view the Needles, afterwards dining with him at Easton Farm, Freshwater. [Pollock, later Sir Frederick, barrister, became a close friend.]

November

2 (Wed) *The Times* reports a speech by the Archbishop of York, William Thompson (1819–90), attacking sensation fiction. AT proposes a rebuttal to champion the morality of fiction but Smith dissuades him.

23 Meets Smith, who donates 10 guineas for the Thackeray monument.

December
Early this month, discussions about starting the *Fortnightly Review*. GHL, approached to edit the journal, at first declines but is persuaded.
 3 (Sat) House party at Waltham with E. F. S. Pigott, journalist on the *Daily News*, and others.
14 Committee meeting of the Royal Literary Fund.
31 Completes *The Claverings* (serialised in the *Cornhill*, Feb 1866– May 1867; book publication by Smith, Elder, Apr 1867). [Critical responses to this and other novels of the late 1860s consistently praised the novelist for what the *Saturday Review* called his 'close reproduction of the actual way of the world' truthfully, humorously and without false conclusions. 'This simple earnestness, this plain sincerity of thought and vision, has a charm of its own which, added to the verisimilitudes of his creations, is what lies at the bottom of the pleasure he gives us' (XXIII [18 May 1867] 638–9). Such is the theme of Margaret Oliphant's 'Novels', *Blackwood's Magazine*, CII (Sep 1867) 275– 7. High marks for artistic writing in *The Claverings* are given by the *Spectator*, XL (4 May 1867) 498–9, and the *Athenaeum*, 15 June 1867, p. 673.]

1865

January
 9 (Mon) Proposes George Smith for membership of the Garrick Club.
18 AT sends 'Notes on the Brazilian Question' to the *Pall Mall Gazette*, Smith's new evening paper, about to be launched. [The work under review was by W. D. Christie, defending his conduct as Minister to Brazil, 1859–63. AT was sharply critical, and writing it he 'fell into great sorrow', for the Christies, particularly Mary Christie (*née* Grant), were old friends (*Auto.*, p. 173).]
30 Begins *The Belton Estate*.
Late this month, Lady Ritchie (Anne Thackeray, 1837–1919), and the Merivales stay at Waltham House. 'I can remember in the bitter cold dark morning hearing Mr Trollope called at four o'clock [more usually an hour or so later]. He told me he gave his man half a

crown every time he (Mr Trollope) *didn't* get up! "The labourer is worthy of his hire", said Mr Trollope in his deep cheerful lispy voice' (*The Letters of Anne Thackeray Ritchie*, ed. Hester Ritchie [1924] p. 125).

February

7 (Tues) The *Pall Mall Gazette* starts publication under Frederick Greenwood's editorship. AT is among its inner circle of promoters led by George Smith and a frequent contributor.

9 First 'Hunting Sketch' published in the *Pall Mall Gazette* (series completed 20 Mar; collected and issued in book form by Chapman and Hall, May 1865).

14 The Postmaster-General at John Tilley's suggestion offers AT a mission to the East, which he declines.

March

This month and the next, active in recruiting staff for a new periodical, the *Fortnightly Review*. Its policy is 'freedom of speech, combined with personal responsibility . . . neither conservative nor liberal, neither religious, nor free-thinking, neither popular nor exclusive; – but we would let any man who had a thing to say and knew how to say it, speak freely' (*Auto.*, p. 162). Articles have to be signed. GHL is to be editor; AT is chairman of the finance board.

29 (Wed) AT at the Garrick introduces GHL to John Tilley.

April

5 (Wed)? Dinner at the Garrick with W. H. Russell, Charles Taylor, Frank Fladgate and George Smith. Taylor (1817–76), contributes a suckling pig from his country house, Beauport, near Battle, Sussex. [Taylor was autocrat of the club, and something of a social model for AT. See *Auto.*, p. 150.]

13 Death of Theodosia Trollope after long illness.

16–29 On leave; goes to Florence to bring Beatrice ('Bice') Trollope to England. He is to engage Frances Eleanor Ternan (1834?–1913) as her music teacher. [See under Oct 1866.]

May

Possibly this month, becomes a vice-president of the Newspaper Press Fund, together with Dickens, Disraeli, Froude, Reade, Tennyson and the minor poet [Martin] Tupper (1810–89).

5 (Fri) Attends evangelical meeting at Exeter Hall for the *Gazette*

and reports back to Smith that he will never attend another. 'You sit four hours and listen to six sermons; – and the sermons are to me (– and would be to you,) – of such a nature that tho' they are in their nature odious and so tedious that human nature cannot listen to them, still they do not fall into a category at which you would wish to throw your ridicule.' Promises one article but no more – 'Suicide would intervene after the third or fourth' (*L*, I, 301) ['The Zulu in London', 10 May 1865].

9   Returns to Smith a cheque in payment for work submitted to the *Gazette*, explaining that it is a matter of principle: 'tho I may well afford to give you any little aid in my power from friendship, I cannot afford to work as a professional man at wages which I should be ashamed to acknowledge' (*L*, I, 301). [This is one of several instances showing AT's meticulous professionalism and fair demands from his trade.]

15 First number of *Fortnightly Review* published, containing first instalment of *The Belton Estate* (continuing until 1 Jan 1866; book publication by Chapman and Hall, Dec 1865). [Some disappointment was registered in the reviews at the novel's tameness, and the charge of repetition was levelled by more than one journal. The *London Review* observed, 'It is time . . . that Mr Trollope should forbear from leading us through the same familiar scenes' (XII [3 Mar 1866] 260). Henry James, in the *Nation*, II (4 Jan 1866) 21–2, found the story 'as flat as a Dutch landscape', but added, 'we have no right to abuse the scenery for being in character'.]

19 ? Dines with Lord Houghton.

23 On postal business in Scotland and Ireland (till 13 June).

June

8 (Thurs) Writes affectionately to 'Bice' from Belfast saying he has received a gift of 10 guineas for her. 'What do you say to a new cow? or perhaps ten guineas' worth of chocolate bonbons?' He signs himself 'Your own affectionate uncle T [for Tony]' (*L*, I, 307).

July

Possibly this month, Lady Ritchie, AT and Rose, and Charles Clifford visit the Millais family.

15 (Sat) AT's review of Ruskin's *Sesame and Lilies* appears in the

Fortnightly, urging Ruskin (1819–1900) to leave preaching to Carlyle, who acts 'almost as a prophet' keeping Englishmen up to the mark. In a letter to his wife Carlyle comments, 'Ruskin's *Sesame and Lilies* must be a pretty little thing. Trollope, in reviewing it with considerable insolence stupidity and vulgarity, produces little specimens far beyond any Trollope sphere of speculation. A distylish little pug, that Trollope; irredeemably imbedded in commonplace, and grown fat upon it, and prosperous to an unwholesome degree' (*Thomas Carlyle: Letters to his Wife,* ed. Trudy Bliss [1953] p. 381).

15–16? William Dean Howells (1837–1920), author and critic, visits Waltham. Howells found his host 'scarcely spoke to him while he was there; and he offered him none of the hoped for help, or advice, as to English publishers, that the young American was too proud to mention' (*Life in Letters of William Dean Howells,* ed. Mildred Howells [New York, 1928] i, 93).

19 ? Meeting with W. W. F. Synge at the Garrick.

August

2 (Wed) Dines with TAT at the Leweses: 'We had a good deal of pleasant talk or rather shouting' (*GE,* viii, 349–50).

3 First of the 'Travelling Sketches' published in the *Pall Mall Gazette* (series completed 6 Sep; collected and issued in book form by Chapman and Hall, Feb 1866).

19–21 Norman Macleod as house guest. Dinner is taken at 6, '(then eaten to get a cigar in the garden afterwards)' (*L,* i, 312–13).

September

4 (Mon) Completes *The Belton Estate.*

17 Goes on leave till 30 October, visiting Germany and Austria with Rose and Fred and meeting Harry at Koblenz; Fred continues to Melbourne, Australia.

November

3 (Fri) Begins *Nina Balatka.*

20 First 'Clerical Sketch' published in the *Pall Mall Gazette* (series completed 25 Jan 1866; collected and issued in book form by Chapman and Hall under the title *Clergymen of the Church of England,* Mar 1866).

30 Dines as Norman Macleod's guest at a dinner marking the

Scottish Hospital's 201st anniversary. He proposes a toast to Macleod.

December

18   (Mon) AT and Rose join the Matthew Arnolds, the Alfred Thesigers and Miss Wynn for dinner at Sir Frederick Pollock's. [The association between Arnold (1822–88) and AT came mainly through the Royal Literary Fund.]

31   Completes *Nina Balatka* (serialised in *Blackwood's*, July 1866– Jan 1867; book publication by Blackwood, Jan 1867). [This and its companion volume, *Linda Tressel*, published anonymously, caused little stir, even when R. H. Hutton in the *Spectator*, xi (23 Mar 1867) 320–30, identified the author from familiar Trollopian mannerisms.]

1866

January

16   (Tues) The Trollopes spend several days at Fryston, Yorkshire, as guests of Lord Houghton. Among the company is Lady Rose Sophia Mary Fane (1834–1921), daughter of the 11th Earl of Westmorland. She notes, 'I wish I had never seen Mr Trollope. I think he is detestable – vulgar, noisy & domineering – a mixture of Dickens vulgarity & Mr Burtons selfsufficiency – as unlike his books as possible.' [Many reminiscences of the novelist record similar surprise at the contrast between the bellowing man and the gentle observer of social manners and the tender passion. Neither judgement comprehends the true character of artist and man.] Rose Trollope appears far more congenial on this occasion: 'a quiet sort of woman & wd be well enough only she has perfectly white hair which is coiffé en cheveux – in the most fashionable way with (last night) a little rose stuck in it wh: looks most absurd' (*L*, i, 321).

21   Begins *The Last Chronicle of Barset*, which he gives the working title 'The Story of a Cheque for Twenty Pounds and of the Mischief which it did'.

27   ? AT hosts a small party at Waltham with the Robert Bells and W. W. F. Synge.

February

3 (Sat) Meeting with George Smith.

9 Attends dinner at the London Coffee House, Ludgate Hill, honouring William Bokenham, Controller of the Circulation Office of the Post Office. Trollope makes a speech.

16 Mr Gibbon and Mr Stoner dine at Waltham.

19 Browning writes to Isa Blagden, 'A. Trollope has invited me to a dinner of the Proprietors and Staff of the *Fortnightly Review*, – I don't know why – for I never gave them a line in my life. Their review or Magazine is very good and respectable, but hardly successful I should fear, as a speculation' (McAleer, *Dearest Isa*, p. 230). [In the event Browning was right. The founders had subscribed £1250 each, but it soon proved that fortnightly issue was unpopular with the trade, so the periodical became a monthly. 'We carried out our principles till our money was all gone, and then we sold the copyright to Messrs Chapman & Hall for a trifle' (*Auto.*, p. 163). The magazine later established itself on sounder footing under John Morley's editorship.]

March

3 (Sat) Proposes Frederick Greenwood (1830–1909), editor of the *Pall Mall Gazette* 1865–80, for membership of the Garrick Club.

7 Dinner at Sydenham with Mr Henry Wyndham Phillips [1820–68] the artist.

8 Lunch with GHL and GE to request GHL not to resign the editorship of the *Fortnightly Review*.

9 AT offers *Nina Balatka* to Smith for the *Cornhill* at a price of £300, stipulating that it should appear anonymously. [Smith declined it.] The Trollopes dine with Mr and Mrs J. E. Millais.

14 10 a.m. meeting at the Athenaeum with H. C. Pennell, Inspector of Sea Fisheries. ?Browning dines with the *Fortnightly* team at St James's Hotel.

April

10 (Tues) After some frank criticism of *Nina Balatka*, John Blackwood advises the manager of his London office, Joseph Munt Langford (1809–84), that he is interested in publishing the novel in *Blackwood's Magazine*. [Blackwood (1818–79), after 1852 head of the publishing house, became a close friend.]

11 Lord Houghton dines with the *Fortnightly* board.

14 John Blackwood offers £250 for *Nina Balatka*.

21 The Pollocks visit Waltham Cross for the weekend. They admire the house, which has 'a *corps de logis* and two wings, one of which held the stables in which Trollope's hunters were lodged, and the other was converted into an office for the Post Office clerks who were under him in his work of superintending the cross-post arrangements of the eastern counties'. AT explains his regular writing schedule of 'two or three hours of the early morning, and he named the number of foolscap sheets of paper which he filled every day'. Pollock surprises him by giving at once a close estimate of the number of words he would have written. Pollock is intrigued by the novelist's methodical way of keeping up a daily calendar of pages completed 'as the days are by schoolboys to show how nearly their holidays are approaching' (*Personal Remembrances of Sir Frederick Pollock* [1887] II, 149–51). [The Pollocks were close friends and neighbours when AT moved to Montagu Square in 1873.]

May

2   (Wed) Attends Royal Literary Fund dinner in Willis's Rooms, at which A. C. Swinburne (1837–1909) is proclaimed as 'representative of that future generation of poets'. In the audience are Charles Kingsley (1819–75) and Leslie Stephen (1832–1904). Trollope proposes the toast 'The Pioneers of Civilisation', with which he couples the names of Viscount Milton and Sir Samuel Baker. [William Spencer (1839–77), MP for West Riding; Samuel White Baker (1821–93), explorer of the Nile.]

9   W. H. Russell is 'ordered' to attend the *Fortnightly* board's dinner at the Star and Garter, Richmond.

11–17   Rose and AT holiday together at Pentre Voelas, Denbighshire, North Wales.

June

During this month and the next, AT acts as editor of the *Fortnightly* while GHL is abroad.

4   (Mon) Dines with the Leweses. Other guests included John Dennis, Alexander Bain (1818–1903, friend of J. S. Mill and Professor of Logic and English at the University of Aberdeen) and Madame Bodichon: 'Bain startled us by his antichristian onslaught, and Trollope amused us by his defence' (*GE*, IV, 266).

15   Assigned to temporary surveyorship of the Western and North

Eastern Districts of London. His headquarters are established in Vere Street post office, near Cavendish Square.

20 AT is offered the post of Surveyor of the Metropolitan District at a salary of £700 rising to £800 in four years, £100 above the ceiling for surveyors. He declines, returning to his district by 8 August.

July

Working at Vere Street on the reorganisation of London postal districts, AT is observed by a colleague 'slogging away at papers at a stand-up desk, with his handkerchief stuffed into his mouth, and his hair on end, as though he could barely contain himself'. [For this and other impressions of AT in the Post Office, see *I & R*, pp. 29–63.]

14 (Sat) ? Dines with Lady Amberley (1842–74), wife of Viscount Amberley, son of Lord John Russell.

August

3 (Fri) Having received a presentation copy of *Felix Holt*, AT warmly congratulates GE and inquires if GHL 'wants any of the new batch of 8000 cigars' just received from Cuba (*L*, i, 346).

19 Dines with Lord and Lady Amberley.

20 AT presses Millais to undertake illustrations for *The Last Chronicle* but without success. [Millais does, however, agree the following year to illustrate *Phineas Finn*.]

22 The *Fortnightly* board meets and agrees to make the review a monthly periodical. [In its new form it first appears in November.]

September

13 (Thurs) AT has to decline an invitation to the Manchester meeting of the National Association for the Promotion of Social Science in October but sends a paper read at the congress, 'On the Best Means of Extending and Securing an International Law of Copyright'.

15 Completes *The Last Chronicle* (published by Smith, Elder in weekly numbers, 1 Dec 1866–6 July 1867; book publication in 2 vols, Mar and July 1867). [Accepted quite simply as 'the best, indeed, the richest and completest' of his works according to the *Spectator*, xl (13 July 1867) 778–80, *The Last Chronicle* crowned AT's achievements in fiction to date. A common

thread among reviews was the very real scare of losing touch with old friends. Thus the *London Review*, xv (20 July 1867) 81: 'Barset has long been a real country, and its city a real city, and the spires and towers have been before our eyes, and the voices of the people are known to our ears, and the pavements of the city ways are familiar to our footsteps.']

Late this month, goes to Ireland.

October

1 (Mon) On leave; goes to Italy and to Paris, where Rose and Henry meet him, for TAT's marriage to Frances Eleanor Ternan. [AT had been responsible for bringing her to Florence as music teacher for 'Bice' (*The Further Reminiscences of Thomas Adolphus Trollope* [1889] p. 41).] Returns home at the end of the month via Paris.

November

9 (Fri) GHL's resignation as editor of the *Fortnightly* is accepted sympathetically and reluctantly: 'I hate the breaking of pleasant relations; and am distrustful as to new relations', but AT recognises that his friend's time 'was too valuable to be frittered away in reading Mss, and in writing civil, – or even uncivil – notes' (*L*, I, 353). [John Morley (1838–1923), later Viscount Morley of Blackburn, became editor from 1867 until 1882 and discharged his duties 'with admirable patience, zeal, and capacity' (*Auto.*, p. 166), although AT did not warm to him personally.]

15 James Virtue (1829–92), successful printer and publisher, invites AT to undertake editorship of projected monthly magazine (eventually called *St Paul's Magazine*). AT is to be paid £1000 per annum and have a free hand engaging contributors. A sale of 25,000, Virtue reckons, will guarantee success. [Circulation in fact was closer to 10,000.]

17 Begins *Phineas Finn*.

19 ? At Brighton.

27 ? Mr Barker dines at Waltham.

December

14 (Fri) Canvassing names for Virtue's new magazine, AT suggests 'The Monthly Westminster' and 'The Monthly Liberal' but deems 'Trollope's Monthly' unsuitable. 'Whitehall Magazine' is another possibility.

1867

Between the years 1867 and 1870, AT's literary career reached its climax, and somehow his way of thinking seemed to undergo a singularly decisive change, which forecast a gradual downward course. From 1860–1 revenues from books had gone on increasing, to reach £2800 for *The Claverings* and £3000 for *The Last Chronicle of Barset*. He obtained £3200 for *Phineas Finn, He Knew He Was Right* and *Can You Forgive Her?* This amount is the highest he received outright for a work of fiction. The last brought in £3525 *in toto*, which sum included half profits on copies over 10,000. The subject of payments is a complex one. AT maintained that the highest rate of pay he received was for *The Claverings* (*Auto.*, p. 197). This was because he thought in terms of units based on the traditional 'three-decker'. For more information on the marketing of his work see Patricia Srebrnik, 'Trollope, James Virtue and *Saint Paul's Magazine*', *Nineteenth-Century Fiction*, xxvii, no. 3 (Dec 1982) 443–63; *L*, i, 240–1, 328–9, 340–1, 367–8; Mary Hamer, *Writing by Numbers, Trollope's Serial Fiction* (Cambridge, 1987).

Other events of the late 1860s signalled a less fortunate future. Contesting Beverley for a seat in the House of Commons was unwise, as was resignation from the Post Office, and hints of uncertainty surround his ventures into anonymous publication and his editorship of *St Paul's Magazine*, undertaken in 1867. Throughout the dynamo of production continued, the social round if anything increased, and by Dickens' death in 1870 AT was certainly eminent among English novelists. From these unsettled years come outstanding recollections of the gregarious, hunting, clubbable AT, including the often-quoted story of the demise of Mrs Proudie. The ebullient Trollope was sometimes perceived in less tolerant light, and letters show a wistful strain that would grow more pronounced in the next decade.

January
11 (Fri) Attends gathering at Painters' Hall, Little Trinity Lane [Painters' and Stainers' Company, one of the City of London livery companies, pioneers in technical education].
15 The Trollopes stay overnight with the Pollocks. Among the guests for dinner are the essayist W. Rathbone Greg (1809–81), the historian J. A. Froude (1818–94), and Charles Herries. Next morning Trollope comes down for breakfast after his usual writing stint at the novel then on hand. He astonishes

the company by saying, 'I have just been making my twenty-seventh proposal of marriage.'

16 Meets James Virtue to discuss editorship of *St Paul's Magazine*.

24 AT formally accepts terms for editing *St Paul's*, a two-year term at £1000 per annum plus a further sum of £75 for the part-time services of a sub-editor. [AT approached Robert Bell for the post.]

February

16 (Sat) ? Sits for portrait photograph by Elliot and Fry, Baker Street.

March

7 (Thurs) Alexander Strahan asks for a title for the latest collection of stories. AT has in mind 'Tales of All Countries, Third Series', but settles for *Lotta Schmidt and Other Stories*. Strahan commits a gaffe by proposing to stretch them to two volumes, incurring the novelist's wrath.

10 AT complains to Strahan about publishing his stories in two volumes: 'I have always endeavoured to give good measure to the public – The pages, as you propose to publish them, are so thin and desolated, and contain such a poor rill of type meandering thro' a desert of margin, as to make me ashamed of the idea of putting my name to the book' (*L*, I, 372). [A similar occurrence surrounded issue of *Sir Harry Hotspur of Humblethwaite* by Hurst and Blackett in 1871. AT thwarted the attempt to bring this short novel out in two volumes, commenting, 'I stood to my guns. *Sir Harry* was published in one volume, containing something over the normal 300 pages, with an average of 220 words to a page, – which I had settled with my conscience to be the proper length of a novel volume' (*Auto.*, p. 289).]

12 After an afternoon in the gallery of the House of Commons, AT spends the evening with the Amberleys. ['Kate', Lady Amberley (1842–74), was well known for her salon; AT was a guest on at least four occasions.]

23 R. H. Hutton in an anonymous review in the *Spectator* unhesitatingly pronounces that *Nina Balatka* is by AT. [Hutton wrote several perceptive reviews of AT's fiction during his long association with the journal.]

April

3 (Wed) Laurence Oliphant (1829–88) taxes John Blackwood with questions surrounding the authorship of *Nina*. Blackwood replies that if asked he should say the author is Disraeli (1804–81).

9 Dines at Lord and Lady Amberley's with T. H. Huxley (1825–95), Lady Frances Russell and E. Knatchbull Hugesson. 'A. and I thought T's voice too loud, he rather drowned Huxley's pleasant quiet voice which was certainly better worth hearing' (*The Amberley Papers: The Letters and Diaries of Lord and Lady Amberley*, ed. Bertrand and Patricia Russell [1937] ii, 27).

12 Death of Robert Bell, whom AT had chosen to be sub-editor of *St Paul's Magazine*. The post falls to Edward James Stephen Dicey (1832–1911), later editor of the *Observer*, 1870–79. [Dicey was paid £250 out of AT's £1000 per annum.]

13 Owing to pressure of work, declines invitation from Edmund Routledge (1843–99) to contribute to his new magazine, *Broadway* (begun Sep).

18 Attends funeral of Robert Bell at Kensal Green Cemetery.

May

Early this month, AT solicits contributions for a memorial fund in aid of Robert Bell's widow. Charles Dickens acknowledges the effort: 'I had heard with much satisfaction that poor Mrs Bell had found a friend in you, for I knew she could have no stauncher or truer friend' (*L*, i, 379).

4 (Sat) Responds to the toast 'The Interests of Literature' at the anniversary dinner of the Royal Academy prior to the opening of the annual summer exhibition.

6 Dines with GHL at the Garrick Club, along with Browning, W. E. Forster, Fitzjames Stephen, E. S. Beesly, George Meredith (1828–1909), Frederick Greenwood and Alexander Macmillan (1818–96). [Beesly (1835–1915), philosopher and educator, shared with AT an interest in Cicero.]

15 At the Royal Literary Fund dinner in Willis's Rooms, Sir Francis Hastings Charles Doyle (1810–88), Professor of Poetry at Oxford, proposes a toast to 'Imaginative Literature and Mr Anthony Trollope'. He says, 'We all of us scramble every week for the new number of the last novel now in progress [*The Last Chronicle*] . . . .' As President of the Fund, Lord Stanhope expresses pleasure at seeing AT's characters reappear in

subsequent novels in the manner of Balzac. AT comments, 'The carrying on of a character from one book to another is very pleasant to the author; but I am not sure that all readers will participate in that pleasure' (*L*, i, 380). [Perhaps he had in mind the conversation he overheard at the Athenaeum that sealed Mrs Proudie's fate. See *Auto.*, pp. 237–8.]

On the same day he completes *Phineas Finn* (serialised in *St Paul's*, Oct 1867–May 1869; book publication by Virtue, Mar 1869). [Diminished enthusiasm greeted this novel, possibly because of its partially Irish connection and the praise heaped on its predecessor. Phineas fluttering among four ladies was less well liked than the political and social doings he was involved in. There was speculation about the real-life models for various characters – notably Mr Turnbull, identified with John Bright. [See under 31 Mar 1869.] Appearance of the novel gave rise to a long essay, 'Trollope's Irish Novels', in the *Dublin Review*, lxv (Oct 1869) 361–7, in which the novelist was praised for his fair and accurate portrayal of the Irish character and nation.]

June

1 (Sat) At Clovelly, north Devon, staying until the 10th.

2 Begins *Linda Tressel*.

13 AT buys the late Robert Bell's library of 4000 volumes before they go to auction. Hearing of the imminent sale at Willis and Sotheran's, AT exclaims, 'This must not be. We all know the difference in value between buying and selling of books.' He pays well above the market price for the collection (*E*, p. 307).

14 Meeting with Frederic Chapman.

July

10 (Wed) Completes *Linda Tressel* (serialised in *Blackwood's*, anonymously, Oct 1867–May 1868; book publication by Blackwood, May 1868).

16 John Blackwood offers £450 for the copyright of *Linda Tressel*. [AT is to explain his two ventures in anonymous publication as an attempt 'to see whether I could succeed in obtaining a second identity, – whether as I had made one move by such literary ability as I possessed, I might succeed in doing so again' (*Auto.*, p. 175). In fact neither *Nina Balatka* nor *Linda Tressel* sold well.] The historian John Lothrop Motley (1814–

77) dines with Sir William Stirling-Maxwell (1818–78), historical writer and treasurer of the Royal Literary Fund, and meets AT.

17 Motley writes home to his wife, Mary, 'I forgot to say that I liked Trollope very much; he was excessively friendly, and wants me to come down to him where he lives in the country – I forget where. Perhaps I shall' (*The Correspondence of John Lothrop Motley*, ed. George William Curtis [New York, 1889] II, 291).

18 Goes on leave till 20 August, travelling on the continent. Rose joins him in Paris; they visit the Engadine Valley in Switzerland.

August
Lotta Schmidt and Other Stories published by Strahan.

September
1 (Sun) Begins *The Golden Lion of Granpere*.

October
1 (Tues) James Virtue's new shilling periodical, *St Paul's Maga-zine*, is launched after a publicity campaign in which AT's name figures prominently. [The opening chapters of *Phineas Finn* get the magazine off to a good start, but the *Spectator* warns on 5 Oct that Trollope must 'throw a little more warmth into *St Paul's*, if he is to be as successful as we hope'.]

9 John Tilley acknowledges AT's resignation from the Post Office (officially tendered on the 3rd): 'You have for many years ranked among the most conspicuous servants of the Post Office which on several occasions when you have been employed on large and difficult matters has reaped much benefit from the great abilities which you have been able to place at its disposal . . .' (*L*, I, 392). [AT later recalled how hard he had worked so as not to skimp on official duties and how the severance had been planned once he had saved enough so as not to miss his pension. While insisting that the timing of his resignation coincided with the workload incurred with editing *St Paul's*, he frankly rehearsed the longstanding disappointments he had felt when he was rejected for the post of Assistant Secretary. He concluded by reiterating his love of

his career, having 'thought very much more about the Post Office than I had of my literary work' (*Auto.*, pp. 239–45).]

18   GE writes to John Blackwood, 'I suppose you have seen in the papers that our friend Mr Trollope has resigned his place in the Post Office. I cannot help being rather sorry, though one is in danger of being rash in such judgements. But it seems to me a thing greatly to be dreaded for a man that he should be in any way led to excessive writing' (*GE*, IV, 392).

22   Completes *The Golden Lion* (serialised in *Good Words*, Jan–Aug 1872; book publication by Tinsley Brothers, May 1872). [Accorded respectable appreciation for its characters and humour, this novel prompted the *Spectator*, XLV (18 May 1872) 630–1, to repeat its view of Trollope as the great 'Social naturalist', although the *Saturday Review*, XXXIII (29 June 1872) 833–5, dubbed the social observation of life in the Vosges as little deeper than might be gathered from 'one or two days spent at an hotel a little out of the main route'.]

31   A farewell dinner takes place at the Albion Tavern, hosted by Frank Ives Scudamore; Edmund Yates is a vice-chairman and proposes a toast. Scudamore makes an amusing speech on how AT struggled to gain his place in literature without ever neglecting his official duties. Returning thanks, AT expresses his sorrow at bidding adieu to the Post Office. The Moray Minstrels entertain.

November

2   (Sat) Over 500 guests, many of them celebrities in literature, art and public life, gather at the Freemasons' Hall for a farewell banquet in honour of Charles Dickens prior to his reading tour of America. AT has agreed to be one of the stewards, though 'Not specially in that set', and he answers the toast to literature in a lively speech turning on a favourite topic, a defence against Carlyle's debunking of fiction. Carlyle is not present. Ladies are seated in the gallery overlooking a magnificently decorated dining-hall with 20 arched wall panels each emblazoned with the title of one of Dickens' books. The British and US flags are prominent. After the banquet AT has a long talk with Laura Hain Friswell, daughter of J. Hain Friswell (1825–78), about *The Old Curiosity Shop* and little Nell. 'His opinion was, I found, very much like my father's, and not at all complimentary to my heroine; but he was exceedingly compli-

mentary to me, and when I said I wondered Mr Dickens remembered me, he replied "he did not wonder at it all; authors never forget those who admire their works"' (Friswell, *In the Sixties and Seventies* [1905] pp. 169–70).

5–12   At Brighton.

13   Begins *He Knew He Was Right*.

15   Virtue agrees to buy *He Knew He Was Right* and bring it out in 32 weekly parts, paying AT £100 per instalment.

30   AT tells an unknown correspondent that he has no present intention of standing for election to Parliament in a certain borough.

December

6   (Fri) Temporarily indisposed by a sore throat.

7   Starts negotiating with George Smith for publishing the Barsetshire novels as a series. [In fact it was not until 1878–9 that such a series appeared, published by Chapman and Hall in eight volumes.]

1868

No event in the year – nor any in the sphere of his personal life since his schooldays – can have been such a trial to AT as his defeat in the General Election of 1868, when he contested Beverley, in the East Riding of Yorkshire; nothing at least can have matched it for the public humiliation to which it exposed him, an eventuality that he had previously carefully avoided. Though he might write to his friend Anna Steele four days after his defeat, 'as for the election, I let that run like water off a ducks back' (*L*, 1, 454), the account in the *Autobiography* tells a rueful tale. It is significant that, recalling the event, he harks back to early days at the Post Office, when his self-esteem was precarious and his uncle greeted news of his political ambitions with sarcasm: 'My uncle was dead, but if I could get a seat, the knowledge that I had done so might travel to that bourne from whence he was not likely to return, and he might there feel that he had done me wrong' (*Auto.*, p. 250). It seems highly significant that his mind should spring back to that condition of the luckless youth born to failure.

Beverley was indeed an unwise and scarring episode. Aided by friends, such as Charles Buxton, he found himself up for Beverley, which had a long and unsavoury electoral record. AT was (in his own words) 'an advanced, but still conservative liberal' with no great gifts on the platform and a burning impatience with committee procedures and the slow unfolding of the art of the possible. Still, burning ambition he had and high regard for the moral responsibility of the politician. As he puts it in *Doctor Thorne*,

> No other great European nation has anything like it [a seat in Parliament] to offer to the ambition of its citizens; for in no other great country of Europe, not even in those which are free, has the popular constitution obtained, as with us, true sovereignty and power of rule. Here it is so; and when a man lays himself out to be a member of Parliament he plays the highest game and for the highest stakes which the country affords. (Ch. 17)

His running mate was Marmaduke Constable Maxwell, son of Lord Herries of nearby Everingham Park, and the retiring Tory member was Sir Henry Edwards, chairman of the Beverley Iron and Waggon Company. At a meeting on 3 November, Sir Henry was vociferously assailed by cries of 'Maxwell and Trollope', chairs were broken and fighting disrupted the meeting. AT behaved with dignity but recoiled from the hornets' nest of politicking, and handed his opponents a stick when he took refuge in hunting to ease his wounded spirit, an activity he found a great deal more congenial than ranting on the hustings. Election day (17 Nov) was worthy of Eatanswill, and the declaration, with Edwards (Conservative) topping the poll with 1132 votes and AT bottom of the poll with 740, was inevitably followed by a petition. This was heard on 9–11 March 1869 by Baron Martin, who found extensive bribery at the municipal elections two weeks before the parliamentary contest. Beverley was disfranchised.

AT speaks with uncharacteristic wrath in the *Autobiography* of his canvassing: 'I was subject to a bitter tyranny from grinding vulgar tyrants' (*Auto.*, p. 258), and he objects profoundly to being used and exploited. Most of all his scrupulous nature recoiled from the discovery that 'political cleanliness was odious to the citizens' (p. 261). The fortunate outcome of all this misery, however, lies in the steely portrayal of chicanery and self-serving politicians in later novels. Something of AT's costly experience is visible in *Ralph the Heir* (1871), *Phineas Redux* (1874) and *The Prime Minister* (1876).

January

4 (Sat) Dines at the Garrick with the distinguished physician Sir Henry Thompson (1820–1924), created 1st Baronet Thompson (1899), surgeon to Queen Victoria. [See under 13 Jan 1874.]

6 Leaves London to go on a hunting trip in Huntingdonshire. Spends about 10 days in the area.

12 At Stilton, Huntingdonshire.

14–?17 At Casewick, country home of Sir John Trollope, soon afterwards created 1st Lord Kesteven (14 Apr). [His grandfather was Thomas Middleton Trollope, a brother of AT's grandfather.]

19 'Bice' Trollope is ill with mumps. AT, greatly concerned, informs her father that she will be well taken care of.

20 Delivers his lecture 'Politics as a Daily Study for Common People' at Stratford, east London. Dines with Charles Buxton (1823–71), liberal politician and hunting crony.

February

5 (Wed) E. S. Dallas notifies AT that *The Vicar of Bullhampton* (sold to Bradbury and Evans for £2500) should run over 32 numbers of the periodical *Once a Week*, which he edits.

12 Dines with Sir James Emerson Tennent (1804–69), Civil Secretary to the colonial government of Ceylon, 1845–50, and author of *Ceylon: An Account of the Island, Physical, Historical, and Topographical* (1859).

13 ? Theatre with Rose.

14–?17 Rose and AT travel to Hastings.

20 'Awfully bad day' hunting at Skreens, near Roxwell, Essex.

29 Accepts commission to conduct negotiations with the US Post Office for a new postal convention. [In the previous December John Tilley had advised the Postmaster-General that the task would need a strong man. Sending AT would meet that requirement, and there would be advantages in his popularity among Americans. AT was also entrusted by the Foreign Office to negotiate an international copyright agreement. This came to nothing. See *Auto.*, pp. 264–7 and *S*, pp. 73–8.]

Henry Brackenbury, later Sir Henry (1837–1914), writer on military topics, visits Waltham Cross from the end of February to early in March. Meets Rose – 'whose beautiful feet made a great impression on me' – and John Blackwood. AT tells him he had decided not to leave the public service until he had made and invested enough

from writing to give him an income equal to what he would lose
by leaving the Post Office. [AT had left the service on 31 Oct 1867.
By retiring eight years before his sixtieth birthday he had forfeited
a pension of about £500 per annum.] Brackenbury notes AT is a
great smoker and sees a wall of his library covered with small
cupboards or bins filled with cigars. [From time to time he tried to
give up the habit.] AT tells how he goes to work in the early hours
and finishes his task before breakfast, and Brackenbury says he
envies his power of imagination. AT replies, 'Imagination! my dear
fellow, not a bit of it; it is cobbler's wax.' The secret was to put a
lump of cobbler's wax on the chair and stick to it until the job was
done (Brackenbury, *Some Memoirs of my Spare Time* [1909] pp. 48–
53). [Since 1861 this had been a favourite conversational gambit,
told with relish and sometimes violent gesticulation towards the
seat of inspiration.]

March

4–6   (Wed–Fri) The Trollopes visit Sir Frederick Pollock. At dinner
      the guests include Sir Frederick and Lady Rogers, Charles
      Carmichael Lacaita, Dr De Mussy and Julia Moore.
17   AT is presented at court by Lord Stanhope, one of 250 at the
      Prince of Wales's levee at St James's Palace.
          Possibly also today, lectures at Bishopsgate for the Revd
      William Rogers, Rector of St Botolph's Church, and founder
      of Bishopsgate Institute (1894).

April

9   (Thurs) Receives instructions for mission to the United States.
11   Leaves Liverpool for the United States on postal mission. His
     pay for the assignment is five guineas per day plus passage
     and expenses. His chief objective will be to secure for Cunard
     the two-way international mail-packet arrangement, running
     between London, Queenstown (Cobh, Ireland) and New York.
22   Arrival in New York. On the point of sailing for home after
     his triumphant reading tour of America, Dickens writes to
     James T. Fields of his amazement at seeing AT coming aboard
     his ship, the *Russia*, in the mail tender to greet him. 'He had
     come out in the Scotia just in time to dash off again in said
     tender to shake hands with me, knowing me to be abroad
     here. It was most heartily done' (*The Letters of Charles Dickens*,
     ed. Mamie Dickens and Georgiana Hogarth [1893] pp. 685–6).

24 Reaches Washington, DC, where he is based most of the time while in America for meetings with Alexander W. Randall, Postmaster-General of the United States, and Joseph Blackfan, Superintendent of Foreign Mails. [From 21 to 23 May he managed a trip to Richmond, Virginia, and at the end of the month he spent several days in Baltimore.]

May
 6 (Wed) In Boston from today till the 14th. Mrs Annie Fields (1834–1915), wife of the publisher James T. Fields, is amused by AT's vehement expressions of distaste over Washington and impeachment [of President Andrew Jackson on 25 Feb].
 8 During negotiations for an Anglo-American agreement on postal rates he is in touch with Longfellow and recommends a place to stay while in London – Mrs Garland's [later Garlants] hotel in Suffolk Street, Pall Mall – 'a place much frequented by country Bishops and Arch-Deacons, and highly respectable'. [AT suffers a stroke at this hotel in Nov 1882.]
18 AT cannot make headway in his postal negotiations, the Americans trying to keep their options open possibly to satisfy their own shipping interests. He reports to Tilley, 'Their public is more patient than ours, and they are less driven than we are in matters of quickness and punctuality . . . it will be useless for me to remain here, if nothing can be done' (*L*, I, 427–8). [Tilley did what he could to enable AT to make a treaty on the best terms he could, urging the Treasury on 8 June, 'It is not desirable to detain Mr Trollope in America longer than is absolutely necessary.' Again on 17 June he wrote, 'Take pity on Trollope and let us have an answer', and 10 days later he was still asking the Treasury for action: 'Trollope himself went out to please me at some inconvenience to himself and he is most anxious to get back' (*Comm.*, pp. 75–6). At last on 1 July Tilley sent AT a telegram: 'Make Treaty on the best terms you can.']
   Also today, Annie Fields writes to Kate Field, 'We had a very pleasant visit from good whole-souled Mr Trollope. A few such men redeemed Nineveh. He always seems the soul of honesty' (*L*, I, 426).
25 Kate Field notes in her diary, 'Met Anthony Trollope same as ever.'
27 Kate Field's diary records, 'Met Anthony Trollope again.'

28 'Anthony Trollope called and went with us to the Capitol', notes Kate Field.

June

3 (Wed) AT is finding Washington intolerable and writes to Kate Field, 'This place is so awful to me, that I doubt whether I can stand it much longer. To make matters worse a democratic Senator who is stone deaf and who lives in the same house with me, has proposed to dine with me every day!' (*L*, I, 432).

6 Kate Field records in her diary that AT stayed an hour or two. He asks her to write a story for *St Paul's*. 'If I can it will be a feather in my cap. If I can't – well, we shall see' (Whiting, *Kate Field*, p. 183).

7 Travels to New York, where he stays until the 16th.

12 Completes *He Knew He Was Right* (published by Virtue in sixpenny weekly numbers, 17 Oct 1868–22 May 1869; parallel two-shilling monthly parts from Nov; book publication by Strahan, May 1869). [Although reviews were on the whole favourable, a perceptible drop in the atmosphere of critical appraisal predicted changes on the horizon. The *Saturday Review*, always on the chilly side where Trollope was concerned, wearily observed that the British Museum might soon have to set aside a room for his collected works (xxvii [5 June 1869] 751–3). Observing that his story was 'as shapeless as a boned fowl', *The Times* went on to patronise his 'wonderful facility of production and indulgence in making his characters think on paper' (26 Aug 1869, p. 4). By and large the subject matter of an unhappy marriage was considered unpleasant; even the *Spectator* (usually so perceptive about Trollope's intentions) found fault with the Trevelyans (xlii [12 June 1869] 706–8).]

15 Begins *The Vicar of Bullhampton*.

16 The *Boston Daily Evening Transcript* carries a description of the novelist: 'He is a strange looking person. His head is shaped like a minnie ball, with the point rounded down a little, like the half of a lemon cut transversely in two. It is small, almost sharp at the top, and bald, increasing in size until it reaches his neck. His complexion and general bearing are much like Dickens's. His body is large and well preserved. He dresses like a gentleman and not like a fop, but he squeezes his small, well-shaped hand into a very small pair of coloured kids. He "wears a cane", as all Englishmen do' (*L*, I, 437).

18 Wilting in the Washington heat, AT informs Kate Field that
    he has written his epitaph. It runs in part

> Washington has slain this man,
> By politics and heat together.
> Sumner alone he might have stood,
> But not the Summer weather.

[Charles Sumner prominent opponent of slavery.] By the name
he adds, 'Very doubtful' (*L*, 1, 433).

July
8 (Wed) AT writes to Kate Field from Washington, 'Oh, Lord
   what a night I spent, – the last as ever was, – among the
   mosquitoes, trying to burn them with a candle inside the net!
   I could not get at one, but was more successful with the
   netting. I didn't have a wink of sleep, and another such a
   night will put me into a fever hospital' (*L*, 1, 437). [At this
   time, far from home and sorry for himself, he writes his most
   flirtatious and affectionate letters to Kate Field. She persuades
   him to see Dickens with a view to getting her short and vivid
   account of the readings published. Advance sheets should
   have been sent to Chapman and Hall for simultaneous publication in America and England, but this had not been done
   and Dickens therefore felt disinclined to see the book appear.
   Kate Field published a revised edition, *Pen Photographs of
   Charles Dickens's Readings* (1871) a year after his death.]
11 The postal treaty concluded on disappointing terms with no
    resolution on the sailing issue and minor changes in postal
    rates. The Duke of Montrose, Postmaster-General, regards the
    mission as a failure but commends AT for his exertions.
13 In New York and then to Boston, possibly visiting Mrs
    Theodore Parker and Mrs Charles Homans.
14 Back to New York.
15 Sails from New York for England, the mission having lasted
    111 days.
26 Arrives home at midnight vowing he will go on no further
    ambassadorial business.

August
10 (Mon) Sets out with Rose for Scotland, where they stay with
    John Blackwood at Strathtyrum, near St Andrews.

19 AT's wild demeanour and boisterous manner offend one of
the guests at dinner, the Revd A. K. H. Boyd (1825–99): 'The
sight of the great novelist was a blow. He was singularly
unkempt, and his clothes were wrinkled and ill-made. His
manner was a further blow. We listened for the melodious
accents which were due from those lips: but they did not
come. Indeed, he was the only man I had heard swear in
decent society for uncounted years. . . . How could that man
have written the well-remembered sentences which had
charmed one through these years' (Boyd, *Twenty Five Years of
St Andrews* [1892] i, 99–101). Of the same holiday another
observer comments, 'The echo of Mr Trollope's laugh seems
to come back to me as I strive to recall his genial presence,
and the incidents of the visit: the walks, the games of golf he
insisted on playing on the Ladies' Links, pretending to faint
when he made a bad shot, his immense weight causing a sort
of earth-quake on the sandy ground . . .' (Mrs Gerald Porter,
Annals of a Publishing House [1898] iii, 198).

25 John Blackwood recalls the Trollopes' visit: 'They were both
very pleasant, and have induced us to promise to meet them
at Inverness on Friday and go to Skye. From the look of the
weather I begin to repent of my promise. He is great fun, and
I daresay we shall enjoy the expedition, though rain and wind
may spoil the scenery.' Recalling their last outing he notes, 'I
had a farewell bathe with Anthony yesterday evening, and
we parted almost with tears at Lake Coruisk.'

September
Possibly this month Dickens writes to TAT, 'Anthony's ambition
[in becoming candidate for Beverley] is inscrutable to me. Still, it
is the ambition of many men; and the honester the man who
entertains it, the better for the rest of us, I suppose' (*WIR*, ii, 128–
9).

October
30 (Fri) Campaigns in Beverley.

November
1 (Sun) Completes *The Vicar of Bullhampton* (published by Bradbury and Evans in monthly numbers, July 1869–May 1870;
book publication, Apr 1870). [Sympathetic treatment of a fallen

woman as a fictional subject did not alarm the critics so much
as the unevenness and tedium of the narrative, *The Times*
declaring it 'as flat as walking along the Trumpington Road'
(3 June 1870, p. 4).]

3   The *Hull and Eastern Counties Herald* reports AT's campaign
attacks on Disraeli's ability to change his tactics to suit the
moment – AT's consistent view of Disraeli as mountebank and
conjuror. If elected Disraeli would perform 'the most beautiful
conjuring trick. It will be hocus pocus, square round, fly away,
come again, up and down, turn a somersault, come down on
his feet, and present you with a most beautiful bill to dises-
tablish and disendow the Irish Church, and very likely to
abolish Protestantism generally' (Arthur Pollard, *Trollope's
Political Novels* [1968] p. 7).

Also today, AT in Beverley to face 'that desperate work of
canvassing, – than which no Life upon earth can be more
absolute hell' (*L*, I, 453).

12   Speaking in the Market Place, Beverley, he confronts the
Conservatism chairman about his statement that Disraeli
would abolish Protestantism: 'Did Mr Trollope believe what
he said?' queried his opponent. 'He was a clever writer of
fiction but he never drew upon his imagination at greater
length than that.'

14   Reporting the exchange the *Beverley Recorder* quotes AT: 'I am
told, with that natural invective which one opponent has for
another, that a great accusation has been brought against me –
indeed since I have been in Beverley I have not heard of any
other. I am told I have been accused of writing books. I will
make a clean breast of it. I do write books (Cheers and
laughter). That's my trade (Renewed laughter). I live by it. If
my opponents can't find anything worse than that, all I can
say is that they don't (Laughter)' (Pollard, *Trollope's Political
Novels*, p. 8).

17   Election day in Beverley. AT is bottom of the poll.

December
Fred comes home from Australia much to his parents' relief, hunts
in the winter but is not settled. [AT regarded 1867 and 1868 as the
busiest years of his life. 'I had indeed left the Post Office, but
though I had left it I had been employed by it during a considerable
portion of the time. I had established the *St Paul's Magazine*, in

reference to which I had read an enormous amount of manuscript, and for which, independently of my novels, I had written almost monthly. I had stood for Beverley and had made many speeches. I had also written five novels, and had hunted three times a week during each of the winters. And how happy I was with it all!' (*Auto.*, pp. 276–7).]

6   (Sun) At Bolton, Lancashire.

27   Begins *Sir Harry Hotspur of Humblethwaite*.

1869

January

21   (Thurs) Rumblings of serious storms brewing over *The Vicar of Bullhampton* occur when E. S. Dallas responds to AT's complaint about a delay in publication date of four to six weeks for the new book. [AT, who prided himself on keeping meticulously to contracts, devotes three pages of the *Autobiography* to his trials with Dallas: 'With all the pages that I have written for magazines I have never been a day late, nor have I ever caused inconvenience by sending less or more matter than I had stipulated to supply. But I have sometimes found myself compelled to suffer by the irregularity of others' (*Auto.*, p. 280).] Possibly today, luncheon with GHL.

30   Completes *Sir Harry Hotspur* (serialised in *Macmillan's Magazine*, May–Dec 1870; book publication by Hurst and Blackett, Nov 1870). [Generally acknowledged as a return to form (reviewers were often capable of yearning for the Barsetshire mode while blaming the novelist for repeating himself), this short novel was recognised by *The Times* for characters 'drawn with a vigour and boldness which have been wanting in Mr Trollope's recent works' (16 Nov 1870, p. 4). The *Athenaeum* called it a 'brilliant novelette' (19 Nov 1870, p. 654) while the *Spectator*, admitting its preference for longer works more in tune with Trollope's genius, decided it was one of his best short tales, declaring Emily Hotspur a character of near Thackerayan power (XLIII [26 Nov 1870] 1415–16).]

February

10   (Wed) Rose, AT and one of their sons (Fred?) attend an amateur performance at St George's Theatre, Langham Place,

by the Belhus Dramatic Corps to raise funds for a lifeboat society. One of the plays, *Under False Colours*, is by their close friend Mrs Anna Steele (d. 1914), who acts in the piece.

15 Keeping up with his usual winter hunting schedule (often three days a week), AT provides mounts for Anna Steele and her brother, Charles Wood.

March
Early this month, viewing pictures at the Cosmopolitan Club by Henry Wyndham Phillips (1820–68), AT is surprised at the amount of work on show but doubts it will command high prices for the widow.

22 (Mon) Receiving what he describes as 'a dolorous letter' from Dallas, AT rages inwardly at being asked to give way yet again on publication of *The Vicar of Bullhampton* owing to a misunderstanding about arrangements for Victor Hugo's novel *L'Homme qui rit*. Confessing to a dislike of Hugo's latter work, 'which I regard as pretentious and untrue to nature', AT fumes, 'The Frenchman had broken his engagement. He had failed to have his work finished by the stipulated time. From week to week and from month to month he had put off the fulfilment of his duty' (*Auto.*, p. 281). [He met Dallas's proposal of publication in the *Gentleman's Magazine* with disdain, and *The Vicar* appeared in 11 monthly shilling numbers. Sadleir notes this as another retrograde step, since 'the day of monthly numbers was over' (*Comm.*, p. 299).]

25 Seeking to make a play from material in *The Last Chronicle of Barset* AT inquires of George Smith concerning the half copyright. [*Did He Steal It? A Comedy in Three Acts* was privately printed by Virtue. It was never performed.]

31 The *Daily Telegraph* accuses AT in a leading article of portraying actual politicians in *Phineas Finn*. The major figure is alleged to be John Bright (1811–89), Liberal statesman and redoubtable spokesman of the manufacturing class. AT repudiates the charge: 'It was my object to depict a turbulent demagogue [the character in the novel is Mr Turnbull] but it was also my object so to draw the character that no likeness should be found in our own political circles of the character so drawn' (*L*, I, 468). [His somewhat disingenuous answer has not been accepted by scholars. See John Halperin, *Trollope and Politics: A Study of the Pallisers and Others* (1977) pp. 72–87.]

At the end of this month, temporarily indisposed and takes to his bed.

April
Possibly this month, calls on Edmund Routledge (1843–99), son of the publisher, George Routledge, to decline writing a story for Routledge's magazine.

4   (Sun) Begins *Ralph the Heir*.
10 Attends a banquet in honour of Dickens at St George's Hall, Liverpool. Lord Dufferin [Frederick Temple Blackwood (1826–1902)] is among the speakers. AT delights over 650 guests by speaking in defence of novels.

(Mid-month) AT is ill.

26 Fred returns to Australia. AT accompanies him to Plymouth.

May
James Virtue transfers the affairs of *St Paul's Magazine* to Alexander Strahan.

5   (Wed) The Royal Literary Fund's anniversary dinner. Reverdy Johnson (1796–1876), US Minister to England 1868–9, responds to the toast to diplomats. AT answers the toast to English literature proposed by Lord Justice Gifford. Literature has become a vast profession, he declares: 'has so grown in spite of what can be said to the contrary by thoughtful or by timid men, by sages or by satirists (Cheers)'. Despite the risks and the small chances of success the writer pursues his trade cherishing the activity. 'The man of letters is not bound to sit through long tedious nights, with his hat over his brows, pretending to listen and trying to sleep (a laugh). . . . It is a glorious and a noble profession. . . .' (Booth, *Nineteenth Century Fiction*, VII [1952] 214).

6   Dickens writes to TAT, 'I saw your brother Anthony at the Athenaeum not long ago, who was in the act of reading a letter from you. He is a perfect cordial to me, whenever and wherever I see him, as the heartiest and best of fellows' (*L*, I, 423).

8   Dines with Millais at the 54th Annual Festival of the Artists' General Benevolent Association at Willis's Rooms; Lord John Manners (1818–1906) is in the chair. [Lord John served as Postmaster-General 1874–80, 1885–6.]

18 In Skipton, Yorkshire.

22 *He Knew He Was Right* ends its serialisation, promoting an enthusiastic communication from Mrs Oliphant (1828–97) at Windsor exclaiming, 'You would be amused if you could hear the hot discussions that go on in this quiet corner of the globe concerning the behaviour of Mr Louis Trevelyan [its main character]' (*L*, I, 470). [The Princeton travel books record a meeting with Mrs Oliphant on 29 July.]

July
15 (Thurs) Meets Henry Johnston (Secretary of Glasgow Athenaeum) at the Athenaeum, Pall Mall, and agrees to lecture on 'English Prose Fiction as a Rational Amusement'. AT refuses to discuss terms, saying, 'Do not speak of terms, when a man has something to say and a suitable place and opportunity are offered him for saying it, that should be sufficient for him.'
24 Amelia Edwards (1831–92), *née* Blanford, minor novelist, comes for the weekend. Millais is also a guest. [In an appreciation of AT long after his death Edwards recalled asking him why he let Crosbie jilt Lily Dale (*The Small House at Allington*). AT replied, 'How could I help it: He would do it, confound him!' – Edwards, 'The Art of the Novelist', *Contemporary Review*, LXVI (Aug 1894) 225–42.]
29 At Virtue's printing house; also meets W. D. Gardiner, barrister.

August
7 (Sat) Completes *Ralph the Heir* (published by Strahan in monthly numbers and simultaneously as supplement to *St Paul's*, Jan 1870–July 1871; book publication by Hurst and Blackett, Apr 1871). [Breadth of character without loss of plot unity was the *Spectator's* theme in praising 'a novel so full of life' (XLIV [15 Apr 1871] 450–3). Other papers took up the central figure's reality, the *British Quarterly Review* observing that 'Sir Thomas [Underwood] and old Neefit [the breeches maker] are not surpassed by Mrs Proudie and Archdeacon Grantly' (LIV [July 1871] 126–7).]
10 At Beauport, Battle, Sussex, home of Sir Charles Taylor.
13 Rose and AT go to Paris. He returns by himself by 16 August.
19 Harry Trollope enters publishing with a third interest in Chapman and Hall, for which his father contributes £10,000. [The arrangement lasted for three and a half years.]

September

3 (Fri) Appears at Beverley Town Hall before a government
commission investigating corruption in the general elections of
1868. Between 24 August and 17 November over 700 witnesses
were heard.

4 Travels to France with Rose, returning 1 October.

October

1 (Fri) The *Fortnightly Review* publishes E. A. Freeman's article
'The Morality of Field Sports'. AT springs to the defence of
his favourite pastime in 'Mr Freeman on the Morality of
Hunting', in the *Fortnightly* of 1 December. [Commenting on
his 'violent passion' for the sport, Frederic Harrison recounted
his experience when escorting a young lady to a meet in Essex
and being taunted by the novelist for deserting the principles
of Professor Freeman and Morley: 'I had taken no part in the
controversy, but it gave him huge delight to have detected
such backsliding in one of the school he detested' (*Studies in
Early Victorian Literature* [1895] pp. 222–3). Freeman (1823–92),
Regius Professor of Modern History at Oxford, 1884–92,
recalling the controversy after the novelist's death, noted, 'I
cannot say that Mr Trollope's article at all converted me to an
approval of his favourite amusement; but it gave me the
very best personal impression of at least one of its votaries'
(*Macmillan's Magazine*, XLVII [Jan 1883] 236). AT defends himself
energetically on the subject in the *Autobiography* with marked
emphasis on the temerity of those connected with the *Fortnightly* to allow such a debate in its pages – 'almost as the
rising of a child against the father' (*Auto.*, p. 166).]

December

4   (Sat) Begins *The Eustace Diamonds*.

7 or 8   Lunch with GE and GHL.

27 At Guildford AT and Rose are guests of W. W. F. Synge.
Lewis Carroll (1832–98), a neighbour, joins the party for a very
enjoyable evening in which charades in dumb-show are part
of the entertainment.

1870

January

16 (Sun) Arranges with the station master at Peterborough for a
horse box to convey two horses to Saxby, Leicestershire, on
the 19th, and three horses from Peterborough to Harlow,
Essex, on the 20th.

24 Delivers his lecture 'English Prose Fiction as a Rational Amuse-
ment' at Hull. Repeats the lecture at Glasgow on the 27th and
Edinburgh on the 28th. While in Glasgow visits his friend
Richard Samuel Oldham (1823–1914, Rector of St Mary's
Episcopal Church, Glasgow, Dean of Glasgow 1877–8).

25 James Virtue informs AT that as an economy measure Messrs
Strahan agree to manage the editing of *St Paul's*. [AT relinqui-
shes his editorship after the July issue. The magazine continued
a downward slide, ceasing publication with the March 1874
issue.]

26–7 Guest of George Burns (1795–1890), later Sir George, a
founder of the Cunard shipping line, collaborator with Sir
Samuel and Sir Edward Cunard in making the steamer line
pre-eminent for speed, safety and comfort. [He owned Wemyss
Bay, commanding views of the Firth of Forth. His son, John
Burns, organised the 'Gaiter Club', which organised walking
tours in Scotland and held an annual dinner. AT was a
member. Dr Norman Macleod was 'chaplain'. An account of
one excursion in the Highlands has AT, Macleod and Burns
making such a rumpus at an inn that an old gentleman
complained to the landlord it was a pity that men should
'take more than was good for them'. He was assured that they
had consumed nothing stronger than tea and herrings. 'Bless
me,' rejoined the old gentleman, 'if that is so, what would Dr
Macleod and Mr John Burns be after dinner!' – Edwin Hodder,
Sir George Burns (1890) p. 335.]

29 Begins *The Commentaries of Caesar*, the task of condensing the
books into one small volume: 'I at once went to work, and in
three months from that day the little book had been written. . . . Latin was not so familiar to me then as it has since
become, – from that date I have almost daily spent an hour
with some Latin author, and on many days many hours. . . .
I do not know that for a short period I ever worked harder'
(*Auto.*, p. 291).

29–30?   Stays with Mr and Mrs John Blackwood at Strathtyrum.
31   Gives his 'Prose Fiction' lecture at the Birmingham and Midland Institute, despite suffering from a severe sore throat.

February
Early this month, William Charles Mark Kent (1823–1902), owner–editor of the *Sun* evening paper, 1853–71, tries without success to enlist AT's help in collaborating with him to restore the fortunes of the newspaper.
3   (Thurs) Engaged with Sir Frederick Pollock in auditing the annual accounts of the Royal Literary Fund.
14   Visited by his doctor.

March
5   (Sun) Dines with Charles Buxton.
10   Progress report to John Blackwood on the *Caesar* – 'very hard work'. Having done the first and longest of the Commentaries, he asks if he should proceed.
28   Blackwood advises AT on the Caesar project 'You have I think hit it off capitally' (*L*, i, 504).

April
12   (Tues) Sir Frederick Pollock entertains to dinner the Trollopes, Baron and Lady Martin, the Douglas Freshfields, the Benzons, Browning, W. E. H. Lecky and Valentia Donne.
15   Congratulating Kate Field on successfully launching her career as a lecturer, AT responds to her inquiry about lectures in England: 'I do not doubt you would have very large audiences; – but they do not pay well. . . . I had a word to say the other day about fiction, and I lectured in four places, receiving £15 in two and £10 in two. All of which information may I hope be useful to you soon, as I should so greatly delight in having you here' (*L*, i, 509).
25   Completes *The Commentaries of Caesar* (published by Blackwood, June 1870, as part of its series 'Ancient Classics for English Readers' under the editorship of W. Lucas Collins).

May
4   (Wed) Lord Houghton is AT's dinner guest at the Garrick.
7   Presents copyright of his *Caesar* to John Blackwood as a token

of gratitude for the publisher's encouragement of his new
sphere of interest: 'I was most anxious, in this soaring out of
my own peculiar line, not to disgrace myself' (*Auto.*, p. 291).

15–25   Rose and AT spend 10 days at Bolton Bridge, Yorkshire –
'the prettiest spot in England'. [It serves as a rural setting in
AT's novel *Lady Anna*.]

21   Before severing connections with *St Paul's*, AT expresses something of his attitude to the work to Austin Dobson (1840–
1921), poet protégé of the novelist: 'I cannot refrain from
saying how much gratification I have had during the last two
years and a half in meeting with two or three contributors
whom I have not known before – (in your case have not even
yet known in the flesh) and as to whom I have felt that they
would grace our literature hereafter' (*L*, i, 522).

26–8   Rose and AT are guests of the Revd William Lucas Collins
(1817–87), Rector of Lowick, near Thrapston, Northamptonshire, 1873–87. Collins notes, 'We like them very much, – him
especially, he was so very pleasant to talk to, and at the same
time so perfectly unassuming. What I like best in Mrs T. is
her honest and hearty appreciation of her husband' (*L*, i, 496).
Collins was to recall enjoyable visits to Waltham House, 'where
he [AT] was very happy, though in a different fashion from
his London life, amongst his cows, and roses, and strawberries,
he delighted to welcome at his quiet dinner-table some half-
dozen of intimate friends. Those who were occasional guests
there remember how, in the warm summer evenings, the
party would adjourn after dinner to the lawn, where wines
and fruit were laid out under the fine old cedar-tree and many
a good story was told while the tobacco-smoke went curling
up into the soft twilight' ('The *Autobiography* of Anthony
Trollope', *Blackwood's Magazine*, cxxxiv [Nov 1883] 557–96).

June

An Editor's Tales (a collection of stories published in *St Paul's*, 1869–
70) published by Strahan.

1   (Wed) *The Commentaries of Caesar* appears to patronising
reviews. Charles Merivale (1808–93), Dean of Ely, 1863, authority on Roman history, acknowledges with thanks 'for your
comic History of Caesar' the copy AT had anxiously sent him.
'I do not suppose he intended to run a dagger into me' (*Auto.*,
p. 291).

29 Meets William George Clark (1821–78), Public Orator at Cambridge, to discuss possibility of Clark writing a volume on Aristophanes for the Ancient Classics series.

July
9 (Sat) Becomes involved with negotiations and editing of memoirs of William Brougham (1795–1886), 2nd Baron Brougham and Vaux, published by Blackwood as *The Life and Times of Lord Brougham* (1871).
13 Meets Lord Brougham at Crawley's Hotel.

August
25 (Thurs) Completes *The Eustace Diamonds* (serialised in the *Fortnightly*, July 1871–Feb 1873; book publication by Chapman and Hall, Oct 1872). [Widely reviewed and generally praised for its vigorous characterisation, the novel even drew the grudging *Saturday Review* into declaring, 'Mr Trollope is himself again . . . though perhaps it is his most cynical self' (xxxiv [16 Nov 1872] 637–8). *The Times*, too, pronounced that the novel could 'fearlessly invite comparison with any of Mr Trollope's earliest and best known novels' (30 Oct 1872, p. 4). A less enthusiastic *Spectator* judged the book depressing and found fault with Lizzie Eustace as a lesser Becky Sharpe (xlv [26 Oct 1872] 1365–6).]

September
6–8 (Tues–Thurs) AT stays at Brougham Hall, consulting with Lord Brougham on his autobiography.
13 Begins *An Eye for an Eye*.

October
10 (Mon) Completes *An Eye for an Eye* (serialised in *Whitehall Review*, 24 Aug 1878–1 Feb 1879; book publication by Chapman and Hall, Jan 1879). [As in the case of the previous novel, general critical opinion was that the pessimistic vein was prolonged, its Irish subject a return to the bleak world of *The Macdermots*. By contrast, the *Spectator* welcomed 'this tragic story of mastering passion and over-mastering prejudice, – of a great sin, a great wrong, and a great revenge', concluding that the novelist had found new powers of imagination (lii [15 Feb 1879] 210–11).]

12–13   ? Invites John Morley to join W. G. Clark as his guest at
        Waltham.
18   Remonstrates with Alexander Macmillan for attempting to
        bring out *Sir Harry Hotspur of Humblethwaite* in two volumes:
        'But the fact is that as one pound of tea won't make two by
        any variance in packing the article, – so neither will a one-
        volumed tale make two volumes' (*L*, I, 532–3). 'I stood to
        my guns. *Harry* was published in one volume, containing
        something over the normal 300 pages, with an average of 220
        words to a page, – which I had settled with my conscience to
        be the proper length of a novel volume' (*Auto.*, p. 289).
23   Begins *Phineas Redux*.

1871

Both 1871 and 1872 were years of adjustments, leave-taking and
travel – travel chiefly to Australia, where the Trollopes were
reunited with Fred. The uprooting was decisive from a domestic
point of view, and AT speaks feelingly about 'the terrible necessity
of coming to some resolution about our house at Waltham . . . the
scene of much happiness' (*Auto.*, pp. 293–4). John Blackwood,
always sympathetic, wrote in March, 'Leaving old Waltham with
its garden & all your comforts & pretty things will be a wrench'
(*L*, II, 542) – as indeed it was. Trollope replied wistfully, 'I have
been trying to do what hunting I could with half a fear that I may
never hunt any more' (*L*, II, 543). But as usual work was to arm
him against anxiety; he lined up a travel book and a series of letters
from Australia; Waltham House was shut up (it being impossible
to find a tenant or sell it in the time available), his large library
stored, and the Trollopes set sail on 24 May.

The Australian tour was exhilarating, with numerous public
engagements sandwiched between arduous travel over sometimes
difficult terrain and the gruelling discipline of journalistic enter-
prise. Making Melbourne his headquarters, Trollope managed to
visit every state and New Zealand, where he and Rose suffered
the rigours of a hard winter. Writing as he travelled, he brought
back the almost completed work in December 1872 well satisfied
with the result: 'the book was a thoroughly honest book, and was
the result of unflagging labour for a period of fifteen months. I
spared myself no trouble in inquiry, no trouble in seeing, and no

trouble in listening' (*Auto.*, p. 300). Its reception at home was very favourable, and even in Australia, where it might have been warmly handled, it was taken as a fair and worthy account.

January

17 (Tues) Lectures at Leeds Philosophical and Literary Society 'On English Prose Fiction as a Rational Amusement'.

19 Addresses the same topic at Walsall Lecture Institute. Stays overnight with William Henry Duignan (1824–1914), solicitor, of Rushall Hall. Leaves behind his umbrella and purse.

20 Repeat performance of the lecture on prose fiction at Stourbridge, near Birmingham.

February

27 (Mon) Alexander Innes Shand (1832–1907), journalist, is backed by AT to become a member of the Athenaeum Club.

March

11 (Sat) Joins J. E. Millais, W. P. Frith, William Longman, Lord Houghton, Lord Derby, Wilkie Collins, Tennyson, Shirley Brooks and others in signing a memorial to Mark Lemon (1809–70), editor of *Punch* from 1841 until his death.

April

1 (Sat) Completes *Phineas Redux* (serialised in the *Graphic*, 19 July 1873–10 Jan 1874; book publication by Chapman and Hall, Dec 1873). [This sequel to *Phineas Finn* was praised for subtle characterisation, the portrayal of Mr Kennedy's mental collapse and Lady Laura's painful subjection claiming attention in the *Spectator*, XLVII (3 Jan 1874) 15–17, and the sunnier portrait of Lady Glencora receiving favourable treatment in the *Saturday Review*, XXXVII (7 Feb 1874) 186–7.]

23 Lunch with GE and GHL at the Priory to meet the celebrated Russian novelist Turgenev. A guest, Lady Castletown, points out to GHL 'what a group of genius and of what variety of genius there was standing in a small circle on that occasion – Tourgueneff, Viardot, Browning, Trollope, Burne-Jones, and Polly' [pet name for GE] (*GE*, IX, 15).

28 Attends private viewing of the Royal Academy Exhibition.

29 Sir Francis Grant (1803–78), President of the Royal Academy, gives the toast 'The Interests of Literature' at the annual

dinner. After alluding to the death of Charles Dickens the previous year he continues, 'I am glad to think we have still among us some others most distinguished in the literature of fiction, if, indeed, the wonderful fidelity and truthfulness to nature which p[er]vade the works of Anthony Trollope can be called fiction. (Cheers.) I beg to propose in the interests of literature, "The Health of Mr Anthony Trollope". (Cheers).' AT responds with graceful allusion to Dickens: 'We have all deplored his loss and we are still deploring it; but it has been felt by most gentlemen of your profession in a very peculiar manner. He was the most intimate and dear friend of many artists, and many of you have taken from his works your sweetest and noblest pictures . . . by no word he wrote did he ever damage a youthful mind, by no word he wrote did he ever harm a human heart. (Cheers)' (David A. Roos, 'Dickens at the Royal Academy of Arts: A New Speech and Two Eulogies', *Dickensian*, LXXIII [1977] 103–4).

May

4   (Thurs) Photographic sitting in Regent Street studio. [A drawing from the photograph accompanies an article, 'Anthony Trollope', in the *Illustrated Review*, 15 May 1871.]

17   Attends Royal Literary Fund dinner at Freemasons' Hall. Responding to the toast to literature, AT reminds his audience that much good work is never permitted to see the light, while 'so much that is comparatively poor and trivial has earned good wages'. He hopes that this truth will 'open the pockets of those to whom fortune has been kind in this race. For, my Lords and Gentlemen, fortune has much to do with it. It is not always the best nor the most worthy that wins this race (hear, hear)' Booth, *Nineteenth-Century Fiction*, VII [1952] 215–16).

24   AT and Rose sail from Liverpool aboard the *Great Britain* bound for Australia after an 18-day postponement – 'an incredible nuisance to us, being as we homeless wanderers are' (*L*, II, 548) [Waltham House had been given up]. During his tour of Australia he writes 11 letters for the *Daily Telegraph*, and the required travel book, *Australia and New Zealand*.

25   Begins *Lady Anna*. 'Every word of this was written at sea, during the two months required for our voyage, and was done day by day – with the intermission of one day's illness – for

eight weeks, at the rate of 66 pages of manuscript in each week, every page of manuscript containing 250 words' (*Auto.*, p. 297).

July

19 (Wed) Completes *Lady Anna* (serialised in the *Fortnightly*, Apr 1873–Apr 1874; book publication by Chapman and Hall, Mar 1874). [After the novel's appearance AT declared that everyone found fault with him for marrying his heroine to a tailor. This issue bulked large in the forefront of the English reviews; American notices split between those, such as *Harper's Magazine*, which found the love story 'of unusual interest' (XLIX [July 1874] 290), and the *Nation*, which decided that 'the author is incapable of representing serious emotion' and that the lovers were very probably his two most boring characters (XVIII [2 July 1874] 10).]

27 Arrives in Melbourne and visits the Victorian Parliament (1 Aug). [For more details of his reception as he toured the country see *I & R*, pp. 178–87.]

August

6 (Sun) Leaves Melbourne on the *Rangatira* for Sydney and Brisbane.

8 Arrives in Sydney and stays one day before sailing to Brisbane aboard the *City of Brisbane*. The *Sydney Punch* waxes lyrical on his arrival: 'As noiselessly as the creatures of your own delightful fancy have stolen into our hearts for years and made their home there, you have come amongst us, the brave master, the kindly magician, the eloquent teacher. The very city seems nobler when we think that you are walking its streets, and that its citizens may look upon one who has given so much happiness to millions.'

11–15 At Brisbane he is the guest of Sir James Cockle, Chief Justice of Queensland.

16–30 A busy schedule of visits by coach to Gladstone, Rock-hampton, Maryborough, Gympie and back to Brisbane; dinner in his honour at Rockhampton on the 24th. A well-known squatter (i.e. grazier) Mr Joyce says he is sure that in no place in Australia would Mr Trollope be more cordially received. He reminds his guest that only 13 years ago Rockhampton was a wild waste, 'the haunt of the kangaroo, opossum and emu'.

In a vigorous response AT declares he is determined to give a just and true account of what he sees on his travels: 'I am here as a listener, and will try and learn, allowing nothing to escape notice.'

September

4 (Mon) Arrives at Ipswich; visits the Grammar School, School of Arts, and Mr Vowles's garden at Newtown; guest of Samuel Hodgson, member of the Queensland Parliament, 1868–70, 1871–2.

5–19 Explores the Darling Downs and visits sheep stations.

7–29 Rose remains with Fred in New South Wales while AT makes his visit to the Darling Downs before returning to Brisbane on the 21st. A dinner in his honour takes place in the Parliamentary Library on the 27th. The *Brisbane Courier* notes on the 16th that his tour 'is as carefully watched and recorded by the press as a royal progress'.

October

2 (Mon) Arrives at Sydney aboard the *Blackbird* and continues by train and buggy to Bathhurst and Gulgong, where he is entertained to lunch on the 14th. Thomas Alexander Browne (1826–1915), police magistrate, welcomes him. [As novelist 'Rolf Boldrewood' he includes a character called 'Anthony Towers' in his novel *The Miner's Right*, in *Australian Town and Country Journal*, Jan–Dec 1880.]

20 Travels to Grenfell and Mortray station to stay with Fred. [Gordon Clavering Trollope (1885–1958) describes how the novelist would sit under a shady tree on the homestead writing his daily quota before breakfast.]

23 Begins *Australia and New Zealand*.

November

Possibly this month, AT is invited one lunchtime to try out a newly launched preserved meat and finds it excellent.

6–8 (Mon–Wed) Kangaroo hunting near Mortray.

9 Leaves for Sydney.

15 Attends public dinner at Bathurst.

16 Arriving in Sydney, he attends the House of Assembly.

December

7 (Thurs) Gives evidence before select committee on the New South Wales Civil Service.

9 Ministerial picnic and boat trip down the Hawkesbury River before leaving Sydney on the *Alexandra* on the 13th, having to miss the wedding of Fred to Susannah Farrand (d. 1910) at Forbes on the 14th.

16 Arrives in Melbourne.

18 Lecture 'On English Prose Fiction as a Rational Amusement'. A dinner in his honour is given by the Yorick Club.

21 Writes from his Melbourne hotel to arrange a meeting at Ballarat with George William Rusden (1819–1903), distinguished Australian government officer, writer and educator. [They become close friends.]

27–31 A vigorous programme at Ballarat and district includes exploring goldmines, visiting the theatre, Chinese quarter, hospital and botanical gardens, and attending a service at Wycliffe Church.

1872

January

3 (Wed) Returns to Melbourne, where he spends a week before embarking on the *Derwent* bound for Tasmania.

13 After stops at Launceston and Campbelltown, arrives in Hobart, where he attends service at St David's Cathedral on the 14th. Tasmania delights him, and he admires the people: 'I do not doubt but that a good time is coming for Tasmania', he writes to Rusden on the 17th (*L*, II, 555).

15 Visits the Court House and watches a cricket match.

February

1 (Thurs) Delivers his lecture 'Modern English Fiction as a Recreation for Young People' in aid of the cathedral building fund before leaving by government schooner at midnight for Port Arthur.

6 Race meeting at Launceston.

8   Expedition to the Chudleigh Caves, a rough journey of about 16 miles.

10 Leaves Launceston by steamer for Melbourne.

11–29 Spends three days in Melbourne before travelling to Gippsland and eastern Victoria, and later to Bendigo.

12 The *Cornwall Chronicle* reports a visit to Corra Linn by the Governor and AT in which their carriage almost overturned when the reins broke on the descent of a steep hill. AT and his friends leaped out simultaneously, the horses were secured, and the carriage wheels scotched while temporary repairs were made.

27 AT writes to GE, 'I am beginning to find myself too old to be 18 months away from home.' He has read the first volume of Forster's *Life of Charles Dickens*: 'Dickens was no hero; he was a powerful, clever, humorous, and, in many respects, wise man; very ignorant, and thick-skinned, who had taught himself to be his own God, and to believe himself to be a sufficient God for all who came near him; not a hero at all' (*L*, II, 557).

March

1   (Fri) Leaves aboard the *Baroda* bound for Albany. At Albany meets Matthew Blagden Hale, Bishop of Western Australia, then travels overland to Perth. From Perth he makes a number of excursions into the countryside. In Perth a reception takes place at which AT is escorted by his host, Mr E. W. Landor, police magistrate at Perth, a distant cousin of Walter Savage Landor. AT causes some disquiet by appearing in ordinary day garb with a blue shirt. His gestures are awkward and a witness reports that he spilled a cup of coffee over the new white silk grenadine frock of the young lady making her debut.

7   Charles Reade (1814–84) writes from London announcing that he has been so delighted with *Ralph the Heir* that he has turned it into a play [*Shilly-Shally* was presented at the Gaiety Theatre for a month from 1 Apr]. He offers to send a prompt copy, 'since you ought to make a good deal of money by it if produced in Australia under your own eye' (*L*, II, 559). [The consequence of this affair was a prolonged feud between Reade and AT. It was claimed that over the whist table at the Garrick they would glare at each other in silence and not say one word even in a rubber. They were reconciled in 1877.]

April

2   (Tues) Leaves Albany on board the *Alexandra*.

6   Arrives in Adelaide for a strenuous few weeks of public appearances, tours of sheep stations and mines.

9   To Houses of Parliament (and again on 1 May).

21 Back in Adelaide, visits House of Assembly.

May

2–4 (Thurs–Sat) Visits to hospital and lunatic asylums, and Adelaide jail.

9–20 Visits to Port Macdonell, Mount Gambier, Hamilton, Camperdown and Colac (arrives on the 16th).

20 Writes home to George Smith in high dudgeon about Reade's adaptation, enclosing a letter for the *Pall Mall Gazette* (published 16 July). He adds, 'I have been journeying about from Colony to Colony till I am heartily homesick'; and he sorely misses his hunting (*L*, II, 562). Returns to Melbourne. G. W. Rusden puts him up for membership of Melbourne Club (20 May) as on several occasions (27 July 1871, 15 Dec 1871, 8 July 1872). Visits Houses of Parliament.

22–4? Guest at Government House Melbourne.

24 Attends Queen's birthday levee and race meeting.

27 The Melbourne *Argus* reports on a hunting spill: 'When last seen the distinguished novelist had acquired some experience of Australian soil which he is not likely to be very triumphantly descriptive over.'

June

TAT sells the Villino Trollope, losing £10,000 in the transaction. The family moves out, and TAT becomes Rome correspondent of the *Standard* in the following year.

1   (Sat) Sends letter to the *Daily Telegraph* (published 6 Aug) concerning Reade's dramatisation of *Ralph the Heir*, which had been attacked for indelicacy: 'I wish it to be known that I am in no way responsible for the play' (*L*, II, 563).

8?   Travels overland to Wangaratta, Albury, Grenfell, with a return to his son's sheep-station at Mortray (?17–21 June) and a call at Sydney before heading back to Melbourne by ship, the *Macedon*, on 4 July.

18 Alfred Tennyson d'Orsay Dickens, fourth son of the novelist, visits Mortray station.

July
7 (Sun) Arrives in Melbourne.
16 Visits Pentridge jail. Leaves Melbourne by train, 17th, for Echuca and the Riverina.
22 Attends election meeting in Deniliquin.
23 or 24? Back to Melbourne for governor's ball.
27 Visits Registrar General's Office. Made honorary member of Melbourne Club.
29 Sails for New Zealand aboard the *Albion*.

August
3 (Sat) Arrives at Bluff *en route* for Dunedin via Invercargill, Kingston and Queenstown. Pausing at Dipton for refreshment, AT remarks that 'a better boiled turkey and plum pudding were never put upon a table' (*ANZ*, II, 327). At Invercargill a Miss Edith Hodgkinson observes AT at a Sunday morning service: 'The stalwart man of letters, whose tread shook the church, as he marched down the aisle to take his seat near the pulpit.' She sees 'a burly, upstanding man with a massive head, made more leonine by the whiskers and beard of old Victorian days, these, with his hair greying, an English complexion as of one living much in the open, and kindly blue-grey eyes to match' (*I & R*, p. 183). Itinerary includes a steamer trip in the company of W. H. Pearson, Commissioner of Crown Lands.
5 Leaves Invercargill; spends a day at Lake Wakatipu.
12 Arrives at Lawrence after an arduous journey between Roxburgh and Tuapeka in heavy snow. At one stage the snow falls so thick and fast that in order to ease the horses AT and Pearson walk through mud and slush the 12 miles to Lawrence. While in the town he visits its Athenaeum. On the leg from Lawrence to Milton, AT twice helps coachman Tommy Pope dig out of drifts, remarking he was 'more at ease with a pen than a shovel'. Rose's petticoats become balled up with snow: 'She was an enormous size, and a wonderful sight to behold' (*I & R*, p. 184). [Newspaper accounts speak of the exceptional severity of the winter of 1872.]
14 The travellers arrive exhausted at Dunedin. [It was said of his trip through Otago, 'he had accomplished a journey few visitors, if any, had ever attempted'.]
15 Scheduled to attend a conversazione celebrating the anniversary of Sir Walter Scott's birth, AT disappoints by his absence.

16   To Christchurch, where he spends about a week before leaving
     from Port Lyttleton on the *Alhambra* for Wellington on the
     26th.
28   Accepts invitation to stay with Dr John (later Sir John) Logan
     Campbell (1817–1912), known as 'the Father of Auckland' in
     that city.

September
'Bice' is escorted to England by the poet Alfred Austin (1835–1913),
close friend of the Trollopes. [Austin's 'The Garden that I Love'
(1894) was said to have been based on AT's last home, at Harting.]
 1   (Sun) After trips via Queen Charlotte's Sound calling at
     Marlborough and Picton, arrives at Nelson, the site 'as lovely
     as that of any town I ever saw'. Continues journey by steamer
     to Wellington. At Horokiwi is the guest of Sir George Bowen
     (1821–99), Governor of New Zealand.
10   Fred Trollope is put on the roll of local magistrates in the
     Forbes district of New South Wales.
13   Arrives in Auckland. Welcomed by the Mayor, AT receives an
     address from Auckland Mechanics' Institute and is made an
     honorary member.
16   Leaves by the steamer *Southern Cross* for a tour of the lakes.
     Rose remains in Auckland with the Campbells till the middle
     of the month while AT explores the interior, visiting Maori
     settlements at Maketu and the Taupo and Waikato districts in
     company of government officials. Captain Gilbert Mair guides
     him through the Hot Lakes areas. AT wrote later with delight
     of bathing in the hot springs amidst the 'welcomings of the
     Maori damsels' (*ANZ*, ɪɪ, 476).
17   The *Wellington Independent* reports on AT's attendance at the
     Assembly to hear Sir Julius Vogel (1835–99), Colonial Treasurer
     and ardent proponent of railways across the country. The
     paper describes AT as 'tall, squarely built, slightly florid faced,
     portly in figure, yet singularly light in his step'. AT shows
     himself alert at all times. 'It is surprising how in half-an-hour's
     conversation you can discover how much he knows of the
     state of affairs. . . . He knows the pictures and interiors of
     middle-class life here, and status and pay of people's servants,
     when they have any, the price of labour, the condition of the
     working man, the cost of living, the rate of rents, the general
     condition and well being of the mass of people. . . .'

26 The *Daily Southern Cross* hopes AT will make New Zealand better known to the British public.

27 Meets Campbell and other dignitaries at Cambridge, North Island.

October

2 (Wed) Banquet given by members of the Northern Club hosted by Sir G. A. Arney (1810–83), Chief Justice of New Zealand. Replying to a toast, AT pays tribute to the rapid development of the country in road and rail; 'a great future awaited New Zealand'.

3 Leaves for home on board the *Nebraska*. At Honolulu the Trollopes have to transfer to the *Idaho*.

November

6 (Wed) In San Francisco. *En route* for New York he visits Utah and calls on Brigham Young, second President of the Mormon Church (1801–77), in Salt Lake City. 'He received me in his doorway, not asking me to enter, and inquired whether I were not a miner. When I told him that I was not a miner, he asked me whether I earned my bread. I told him I did. "I guess you're a miner", said he. Then he turned upon his heel, went back into the house, and closed the door' (*Auto.*, pp. 300–1).

25 Arrives in New York, leaving for England on the 27th.

December

17 (Tues) Arrives home; takes lodgings at 3 Holles Street before buying a house, 39 Montagu Square.

20 Reacting to a bout of workers' strikes leading to rises in the cost of living, AT informs a friend that if he cannot smoke a small cigar for under eightpence he will take to a pipe. Since the price of coal had doubled, he vowed to do without. 'Tea and toast at the club for sixpence seems to be the only cheap thing left and I shall live upon that' (*L*, ii, 574).

22 Has resumed hunting with his old vigour. This day spends nearly three hours after the same fox – 'the biggest bellyful of hunting I ever had in life' he writes. 'I never had such a day before. Buff carried me through it all as well as ever. But was *very tired*. He and a second horse I had out were both too tired to be got home. You will be sorry to hear that Banker and another of my small lot are laid up with coughs. I have four

in all' (*L*, II, 574). [The horses Banker and Buff are named in
Ralph the Heir, ch. 27. Mrs M. Evangeline Bradhurst, grand-
daughter of AT's friend Lady Wood (1802–79), described the
horses as 'more like coach horses than anything else, but his
huge squat bulk required weight carriers, and they were safe
conveyances and clever fencers over the trappy Essex ditches'.
Always in the best of spirits on hunting mornings, he would
talk to his garments as he searched for different items of his
kit: 'Now, Mr Top Boot, where is your twin? Can't go hunting
alone, you know.' He would sing in an out-of-tune guttural
voice, 'A-hunting we will go, ho! ho!' with a delighted bellow
on the final 'ho!' And at breakfast he would urge the children
to eat heartily with 'no-one-can't-go-hunting who don't eat a
good breakfast' – Bradhurst, 'Anthony Trollope, the Hunting
Man', *Essex Review*, XXXVIII (1928) 186–7.]

24 J. M. Langford informs John Blackwood that Harry Trollope
has suddenly gone to Australia, and that he should not allude
to it. 'It will be attributed no doubt to a business quarrel but
the cause is one which has troubled our sex from the earliest
periods and the young man has shown himself amenable to
reason and obedient to parental authority' (*L*, II, 575).

1873

January
Early this month, Rose and AT attend a performance of W. G.
Wills's play *Charles I* at the Lyceum theatre. [The play, with Henry
Irving and Isabel Bateman, was an outstanding success.]

 1 (Wed) Lunches with GHL. GHL's diary entry refers to AT's
'trouble with Harry wanting to marry a woman of the town'
(*GE*, v, 357).

 4 Shirley Brooks (1816–74), editor of *Punch* 1870–4, records,
'Anthony Trollope was one of the guests last night [at a *Punch*
dinner?]. He roars more than ever since Australia. He was
exceedingly jolly and Billy Russell was opposite to him so they
fired away good stories. When we were at cards we heard
Anthony's thunder, and then a wild Banshee cry from the
Irishman, till we threatened them with the police. Then
Anthony said we were conventional tyrants, and Russell said

in a weeping voice that Ireland was accustomed to be trampled on' (G. S. Layard, *A Great Punch Editor: Being the Life, Letters and Diaries of Shirley Brooks* [1907] p. 526).

12 Hunting with friends of the Essex Foxhounds, notably Col. Samuel Lloyd Howard (1827–1901), of Loughton, Essex, JP and Deputy Lieutenant of the county. AT's passion for the sport is even more insatiable after 20 months away from England. 'I got home in December 1872, and in spite of any resolution made to the contrary, my mind was full of hunting as I came back. No real resolutions had in truth been made, for out of a stud of four horses I kept three, two of which were absolutely idle through the two summers and the winter of my absence. Immediately on my arrival I bought another, and settled myself down to hunting from London three days a week' (*Auto.*, p. 301). [For contemporary accounts of AT hunting see *I & R*, pp. 112–20.]

15 Completes *Australia and New Zealand* (published by Chapman and Hall, Feb 1873).

February

1 (Sat) Despite frosty conditions, hunting continues, in North Bucks. with William Selby Lowndes (1807–86), Master of the Whaddon Chase. At Leighton Buzzard there is deer hunting with Baron Meyer Amschel de Rothschild (1818–74); 'riding with his hounds was very good' (*Auto.*, p. 301). Having decided on the house in Montagu Square, AT asks Frederic Chapman for payment by bill at 30 days for *The Eustace Diamonds* so that he can pursue the purchase. Interior decoration and furnishing occupy his attention over two months.

(Mid-month) More hunting in Lincolnshire.

17 Rose visits the Blackwoods for a short visit: 'She is looking well and gave a very amusing account of her experiences of American and Australian travelling. Anthony seems to be flourishing and hunting. What an indefatigable fellow he is.'

18 Has secured election of G. W. Rusden to the Garrick.

26 Guest of the Rothschilds at their Buckinghamshire estate, Mentmore Heights, near Leighton Buzzard.

March

2 (Sun) Visits the Leweses. 17 other visitors also present.

April

Moves to 39 Montagu Square. 'Our first work in settling here was to place upon new shelves the books which I had collected round myself at Waltham. And this work, which was in itself great, entailed also the labour of a new catalogue' (*Auto.*, p. 303). [The catalogue is now in the Victoria and Albert Museum.]

4   (Fri) Hunting over for the season. 'In some coming perfect world there will be hunting 12 months in the year' (*L*, II, 585).

21   Still smarting from Reade's adaptation of his novel *Ralph the Heir* for the stage, AT responds to a request from John Hollingshead (1827–1924), manager of Gaiety Theatre, for support in a bid to extend copyright protections: 'If a dramatist have a property in the plot of his play or a novelist in the words of his story, why should not the novelist have a similar property in his plot? . . . I do not think that I should refuse the use of a plot to any respectable dramatist who might pay me the compliment of asking for it. But I do feel very bitter against those who endeavour to palm off as their own the work of others' (*L*, II, 587).

May

1   (Thurs) Begins *The Way We Live Now*.

3   Committee meeting of the Garrick Club.

23   84th anniversary dinner of the Royal Literary Fund in Freemasons' Hall, with Gladstone (1809–98) in the chair. In reply to a toast to the House of Commons, John Walter declares, 'I do think it may well make the humblest member of Parliament content with his lot and console those who are most oppressed with the cares of office, to be told, as we have lately been by a distinguished member of this Brotherhood – Mr Anthony Trollope – in his interesting work on our Australian Colonies, that he looks on a seat in the House of Commons as the highest honour which can be conferred on an Englishman' (*The Times*, 29 May 1873, p. 12, cited in *L*, II, 586n).

24   Visits Lady Stanley of Alderley, widow of the 2nd Lord Stanley, Postmaster-General 1860–6. [Henrietta Maria Stanley (1807–95) was a prominent hostess, and AT was her guest on at least six occasions.]

25   At the Leweses', guests besides AT include R. F. Burton; the artist Philip Hermogenes Calderon (1833–98); F. J. de

Rothschild (1839–98); A. J. Russell (1825–92), MP for Tavistock; F. T. Palgrave (1824–97), critic and poet.

June

1 (Sun) Begins *Harry Heathcote of Gangoil*.

10 Wilkie Collins (1824–89) meets Kate Field at the Trollopes' new London home. Accepting the invitation Collins says, 'Yes I have heard of the American lady – she is adored by everybody, and I am all ready to follow the general example' (*L*, II, 589).

11 ? Browning and John Bidwell come to dinner.

28 Completes *Harry Heathcote of Gangoil* (published as the Christmas number of the *Graphic*, 25 Dec 1873; book publication by Sampson Low, Oct 1874). [The Australian setting took reviewers by surprise and its novelty generally appealed, although the *Westminster Review* regarded it as Trollope's attempt to produce a boys' adventure yarn. The consensus was that the novel was slight but pleasant.]

July

Calls often on Kate Field, who is enjoying much social success in her London season.

1 (Tues) Receives invitation from Lady Cordelia Maria Trollope (1822?–1909), second wife of General Sir Charles Trollope (1808–88) for the 3rd.

3 Resumes *The Way We Live Now*.

7 Hosts a dinner at the Garrick Club in honour of the poet Joaquin Miller. Other guests include Mark Twain (1835–1910), Sidney Lee, Tom Hughes (1822–96) and the Hon. Frederick Leveson-Gower (1819–1907), brother of Lord Granville. Twain feels rather out of things, because AT and Hughes address their talk to 'him of the noble blood', so that he feels himself to be 'at a religious service'. He also notes that Miller and Trollope talked 'both at the same time, Trollope pouring forth a smooth and limpid and sparkling stream of faultless English, and Joaquin discharging into it his muddy and tumultuous mountain torrent, and, – Well, there was never anything just like it except the Whirlpool Rapids under Niagara Falls' (Bernard de Voto, *Mark Twain in Eruption* [New York, 1941] pp. 330–3). [Cincinnatus Hiner 'Joaquin' Miller (1839–1913), poet known as 'the Oregon Byron', left no note of the meeting but did recall a riding episode with AT and Lord Houghton

which turned into a contest. 'One morning Trollope hinted
that my immunity was due to my big Spanish saddle which I
had brought from Mexico City. I threw my saddle on the grass
and rode without so much as a blanket. And I rode neck to
neck; and then left them all behind and nearly every one
unhorsed' – *Joaquin Miller's Poems* (San Francisco, 1909–10) IV,
154, cited in *L*, II, 591.]

13   Leaves with Rose for a 10-day visit to Scotland, staying at
      Inverness.

23   Lionel Grimston Fawkes (1849–1931), amateur artist, breakfasts
      with AT. [He is to illustrate *The Way We Live Now*.] AT dines
      with Fawkes's uncle, Mr Pain, the following evening.

August

19   (Tues) On holiday in Killarney with Rose. He returns to
      London on 30 September very troubled with deafness in one
      ear.

October

Austin Dobson publishes *Vignettes in Rhyme and Vers de Société* with
a dedication to Anthony Trollope.

25   (Sat) At the Garrick Club, shouts at Shirley Brooks that the
      Graphic artist, 'not being able to draw horses, has introduced
      a picnic with champagne into the middle of a chapter about a
      fox chase'. [Brooks died next March. AT, the playwright Tom
      Taylor (1817–80), W. P. Frith and Millais organised a memorial
      requesting a civil pension for his widow.]

31   ? The artist Alfred Elmore (1815–81) comes to dine.

November

13   (Thurs) Guest of honour at a prize-giving to students of
      Liverpool Institute. Before presenting the prizes he praises the
      directors for recognising the value of literary amusements as
      well as literary work in their inviting him to preside. It was
      impossible to exaggerate the effects on the minds of the rising
      generation of works of the imagination: 'They were the
      sermons of the present day, or, at any rate, the sermons which
      were listened to with the most rapt attention.'

Possibly late this month, Lady Monkswell, dining with Mrs
Merivale, meets Trollope, 'who is pleasanter out hunting than in a

drawing room. Mrs Freeman, *née* Merivale, is exactly like the erratic Herman in petticoats.'

December

20 (Sat) A dinner and whist party at Montagu Square. Among the guests is the Hon. Robert Grimston (1816–84), fourth son of the 1st Earl of Verulam and a devotee of hunting. AT has been hunting but is laid up temporarily with a sprained foot after a fall.

22 Completes *The Way We Live Now* (published by Chapman and Hall in monthly numbers, Feb 1874–Sep 1875; book publication, June 1875). [Its pessimistic tone antagonised most critics, dismayed by the pervasive vice exposed in society. Thus Meredith Townsend (1831–1911) in the *Spectator*, xlviii (26 June 1875) 825–6, bewailed its 'atmosphere of sordid baseness which prevents enjoyment like an effluvium. . . . There is not a decently honest man in the book who is not a fool, except the squire, Roger Carbury, and he is an overbearing prig.' The most sympathetic voice came from *The Times*, praising its fairness and objectivity as 'only too faithful a portraiture of the manners and customs of the English at the latter part of this 19th century' (24 Aug 1875, p. 4).]

1874

January

Some time this month, dines with Oliver Wendell Holmes and Thomas Hughes (1822–96).

13 (Tues) Invited to a ball by a friend of his niece, Florence Bland, AT declines graciously: 'You only offer to put me in a corner to play cards! If you had promised to dance three round dances with me I should have come at once' (*L*, ii, 605).

On the same day, a meeting at the home of Sir Henry Thompson. AT is one of 16 eminent people who sign a document in favour of cremation. Other signatories include Shirley Brooks, J. E. Millais, the illustrator John Tenniel (1820–1914) and T. Spencer Wells. [Cremation became legal in 1884. AT's concern with the whole question of dying with dignity crops up in later correspondence; he had a horror of living on incapacitated. Euthanasia is raised in his novel *The Fixed Period* (1882).]

February
2 (Mon) In support of Hughes's bid for Liberal candidacy, AT puts the case to Henry James, Gladstone's Attorney-General. The battle between Hughes and Daniel Grant rages until 1.30 a.m., when James declares against Hughes. [Henry James (1828–1911) became Lord James of Hereford and was a friend at whose shooting box in the country, according to Escott, AT had opportunities of studying political figures.]

March
8 (Sun) Calls on the Leweses in the afternoon. Among the guests are Sir James and Lady Colville, William Allingham, Edmund Gurney, Thomas Woolner, Mr and Mrs Frederic Harrison, George Augustus Simcox, John Ferguson McLennan and Charles Lewes. [The Positivist writer Harrison (1831–1923) was one of AT's collaborators in the *Fortnightly Review*.]
10 Dines with Lady Stanley.
16 ? Hunting in Essex.

April
2 (Thurs) Begins *The Prime Minister*.
17 Starts for Paris (returns on the 30th).

June
4 (Thurs) Invited to join the Reform Club but declines, being already a member of the Garrick, Athenaeum and Cosmopolitan.

July
22 (Wed) Attends Lord Mayor's dinner at Mansion House. Mrs Oliphant notes that Matthew Arnold, 'Anthony Trollope, Tom Hughes, Charles Reade, and myself were the sole representatives of literature (barring the press) that I could see; but oh my ladies of the Opera, how fine they were' (*Autobiography and Letters of Mrs M. O. W. Oliphant*, ed. Mrs Harry Coghill [1899] p. 245).
23 Goes abroad with Rose to Switzerland, returning home on 16 September. During the trip they stay at Lucerne.

September
Harry, who has lately been living in Germany, visits for a short holiday in the middle of the month.

15   (Tues) Completes *The Prime Minister* (published by Chapman
      and Hall in monthly numbers, Nov 1875–June 1876; book
      publication, June 1876). [Confessing to having been hurt by
      the *Spectator* review (a rare admission), the author judged the
      book 'worse spoken of by the press than any novel I had
      written' (*Auto.*, p. 309), and, indeed, comments were harsh in
      several quarters. The *Spectator* review, by Townsend (not
      Hutton as Trollope thought), took issue with the novel's
      vulgarity, by which it really meant the reduction of human
      nature to baser rather than ennobling principles (XLIX [22 July
      1876] 922–3). More or less the same tune was played by the
      Saturday Review, with the damning observation that the old
      hand was losing its cunning (XLII [14 Oct 1876] 481–2). A more
      cheerful note came from *The Times* with reference to real-life
      characters, particularly the sensitive portrayal of the Duke of
      Omnium and his consort (18 Aug 1876, p. 4).]

24   *The Times* publishes AT's views on rail travel between London
      and Basle, which raises issues about baggage costs, inconven-
      ient changes and poor refreshment service. He also relates an
      unfortunate incident when a conductor dropped one of his
      ticket books down the window frame of his compartment.
      Despite reassurances that duplicates would be issued, AT
      ended up having to pay to replace his tickets.

26   Gleefully the *Saturday Review* takes up the story of railway
      misadventure and admonishes AT for not having held on to
      his book and torn the tickets out himself. As for his complaint
      about luggage, he ought to have carried it into the compartment
      himself.

28   AT returns in *The Times* to the matter of inconvenience to
      passengers on the Luxembourg route: 'I submit that . . . a
      gentleman with two ladies, as was my case, could hardly take
      a hundredweight and a half [of luggage] with him into his
      compartment.'

October
12   (Mon) Begins *Is He Popenjoy?*

November
Heavily occupied with hunting.
 3   (Tues) ? Rhoda Broughton (1840–1920) has lunch with the
      Trollopes. [Miss Broughton was a talented authoress of such

novels as *Not Wisely, but Too Well* and *Cometh up as a Flower*, both published in 1867 and branded as fast. AT rather took to her and encouraged her when she was being heartily abused by the critics.]

11 Meeting with Frederic Chapman.

December

4 (Fri) Proposes Percy Fitzgerald for membership of the Garrick. [Fitzgerald (1829–1925), barrister and minor author, friend of Dickens, founder of the Boz Club, acknowledged later, 'He was my sponsor at the Club, and took much trouble about me. He was good enough to say that I was "safe".' Recalling AT's boisterous mask, Percy Fitzgerald thought it 'assumed to hide either shyness or a certain feeling of not being at his ease' (Fitzgerald, *The Garrick Club* [1904] p. 79).]

15 Attends a meeting in London and returns home with a bad sore throat.

16 Ill health and wintry conditions cause him to cancel a visit to an Oxford Gaudy where he was to have been the guest of James Edwards Sewell (1810–1903), Warden of New College, 1860–1903.

1875

The major event of the year was another exhausting journey, AT's second to Australia, which took him via Italy, Aden and Ceylon on the outward journey, and home via New Zealand, Hawaii, San Francisco and New York. The focus of this trip was personal: the wish to spend some time with Fred at his sheep station in Mortray, New South Wales. At the same time writing went on unabated, and as he travelled he took the opportunity of reviewing earlier experiences described in *ANZ* and reporting on this journey in letters to the *Liverpool Mercury*, available in *The Tireless Traveller: Twenty Letters to the Liverpool Mercury*, ed. Bradford Booth (Berkeley, Calif.: University of California Press, 1941). The articles, aimed at potential emigrants, show an enlightened attitude towards English colonialism, paternalism and indigenous tribes and customs. Take, for example, his general reflections on colonisation:

The land becomes ours with its fatness – and the people disappear. . . . It is terrible to think of this extermination. The Maoris are going. The blacks of Tasmania have perished to the last man. The aborigines of Australia are perishing in part, and are partly being driven into the barren interior of their own country. All which seemed to be theirs by as good a title as that which gives any English gentleman his land has been taken from them, for the most part ruthlessly. (Letter xi, pp. 124–5)

AT travelled chiefly in Western Australia, Victoria and New South Wales, after which he visited Hawaii and the United States.

January
6   (Wed) AT has been laid up with a severe liver complaint. 'I am so weak that I can only just crawl', he writes to John Blackwood. 'But I am attaining to a slow but manly desire for mutton chops and sherry, and am just beginning to think once again of the glories of tobacco' (*L*, ii, 642).
Within the week he is hunting again.
10   ? Guests for dinner include Frederick Locker (1821–95), later Locker-Lampson, and Austin Dobson, both popular writers of light verse.
16   Hunting with the Essex Foxhounds AT has a bad fall. An eyewitness describes the scene: 'You could not get at the brook to fly it; but I thought I saw my way to get into the brook through a little coppice. I jumped into the coppice safely; but they had been making a drain just inside the hedge, and Trollope's horse put his feet into it, pitched Trollope over his head, and he lay on his back with his head close to the horse's front feet. In his first plunge to get out he got half-way over Trollope, and we had great difficulty in preventing him doing serious damage' (R. F. Ball and T. Gilbey, *The Essex Foxhounds* [1896] p. 162). [Trollope's antics in the saddle were well known; he was 'reckless enough to ride at a gate while it was being opened' – F. Anstey, *A Long Retrospect* (1936) p. 267.]

February
2   (Tues) Calls on Nicholas Trübner (1817–84), well-known publisher, author and scholar. [He was to arrange publication of the letters about AT's next marathon journey referred to in the headnote.]

16 Recommends to Octavian Blewitt (1810–84), Secretary of the Royal Literary Fund 1839–84, that a grant be made to Jane Mill, a minor writer.

March

1 (Mon) Leaves London for Australia, via Brindisi and Ceylon.
4 In Rome, after an arduous journey during which snowstorms caused delay at Bologna.
5–7 Accompanied by TAT, visits Naples and enjoys vigorous sightseeing walks and a trip to Pompeii.
7 Sails from Naples aboard the *Nigani* with a landfall at Alexandria on the 11th, followed by a day's travel across desert before embarking at Suez aboard the Cunard vessel *Peshawar*. Rose meanwhile travels to Hamburg and Dresden.
17 As his ship nears Aden, AT encounters 'the dreaded heats of the Red Sea'. With a large cabin to himself he has had a writing desk set up and maintains a steady writing schedule. His greatest misfortune so far has been the smashing of an ink bottle inside his suitcase, soaking three shirts and a hundred cigars. Aden he finds 'parched, scorched, burnt, a place of cinders and fire', but he enjoys seeing the tanks (man-made reservoirs) by moonlight.
27 *En route* to Australia AT stays (until 12 Apr) with Sir William Gregory in Ceylon. Entering by the Point de Galle, he travels to Colombo by night coach. From Colombo he goes by rail to Kandy and the gardens of Peradeniya; he visits the health resort of Nuwara Eliya, covering the last 10 miles without a guide in pitch darkness. While there joins an elk hunt. Explores the coffee districts of Dimbula before returning to Colombo.

May

3 (Mon) Completes *Is He Popenjoy?* (serialised in *All the Year Round*, 13 Oct 1877–13 July 1878; book publication by Chapman and Hall, Apr 1878). [General opinion was that this novel was none too pleasant reading. R. F. Littledale in the *Academy* was among those who saw a darker vein in Trollope's writing, judging this work a satire demonstrating 'how very slight are the barriers which part modern civilization from ancient savagery' (8 June 1878, p. 505). The *Saturday Review* also detected a bleaker tone: 'The author used to be fond of his characters; but such lovingness finds no place here' (xlv [1

June 1878] 695–6). Even the *Spectator* perceived a somewhat unwholesome aspect to the novel (LI [5 Oct 1878] 1243–4).]

4 Arrives at Melbourne on the mail steamer *Golconda*, *en route* to Fred's sheep station at Mortray. [For commentary on his second visit to Australia, see *I & R*, p. 185.]

13 At Melbourne.

14 Leaves for Sydney, arriving on the 17th.

18 Attends farewell lunch on Port Jackson Heads, Sydney, for the New Guinea Scientific Expedition led by William Macleay (1820–91), later Sir William, member of the New South Wales Legislative Assembly. This expedition to obtain specimens for the New South Wales Museum is the subject of one of AT's travel letters dealing with the general question of colonisation by Britain. [In typically fair-minded fashion, he drew attention to the dangers of exploiting native peoples and the threats to indigenous rights and traditions posed by annexing powers.]

19 The *Sydney Morning Herald* reports AT's speech at the luncheon: 'He [AT] had been well pleased to be there amongst them, enjoying as they did the well-merited honours he saw paid to Mr Macleay; but the manhood had been suddenly taken out of him by the "side" blow dealt at him by their distinguished friend, Mr Robertson. (Laughter.) In those words which he had incautiously written, and which now rose up in judgment against him, he had not been directly thinking of New South Wales, and most certainly not thinking of the Hon. John Robertson, Premier of the colony. (Roars of laughter.) The general reticence of the Premier was so well-known to them all that to apply to him an imputation of a desire to "blow" [boast] was simply preposterous. (Renewed merriment.) And yet he did repent him of those words, thinking that in any case the colony could not sound her trumpet too loudly in the praise of Mr William Macleay.'

24 Accompanies the Governor of New South Wales at a review of military forces of the colony on the Queen's birthday.

From late this month till mid-July, with Fred and his family at Mortray, writing for four hours a day, riding after sheep, chopping wood and sharing in the life of the station.

June

4 (Fri) Begins *The American Senator*.

30 Writing to Millais, AT describes his routine: 'I eat a great deal

of mutton, smoke a great deal of tobacco, and drink a moderate amount of brandy and water. At night I read, and before work in the morning I play with my grandchildren. . . . I shall be miserable when I leave him [Fred] because I do not know how long I can look forward to seeing him again without again making this long journey. I do not dislike the journey, or the sea, or the hardship. But I was 60 the other day, and at that age a man has no right to look forward to making many more voyages round the world' (*L*, II, 659).

July

3 (Sat) First of 20 letters on his travels published in the *Liverpool Mercury* (continued weekly until 13 Nov 1875).

August

6 (Fri) Appears on the platform at the O'Connell Centenary Celebration in Sydney.

21 Shortly before his departure for England AT is guest of honour at a picnic attended by distinguished figures of New South Wales society. The party travels by special train from Redfern and by steam launch up the Nepean and Warragamba rivers. The Chief Justice, Sir James Martin (1820–86), Premier of New South Wales 1863–5, 1866–8, 1870–2, proposes AT's health in warm terms: 'Wherever, gentlemen, throughout the world, our great British tongue is spoken, there our guest, who has done us the honour to accept our hospitality to-day, is known, admired, and loved as the most popular of modern English novelists. On his last visit to us he applied his great powers of observation to the condition and circumstances of these Australian colonies; and although he may have, in the estimation of some, drawn too flattering a picture of our qualities . . . and may have displeased others by his manly outspoken frankness, there can be but one opinion that he produced the very best book on Australia that has ever been published. (Loud cheers.)' In reply AT observes, 'Not one of you, gentlemen, knows better than myself, the defects of that book; but it is an honest book. It betrays no confidences, I am certain. It wounds no sensibilities; it contains nothing of which I feel ashamed, and I am sure it contains nothing which could give any human being pain. Gentlemen, among the precious recollections of my life I shall cherish the friendships which I

have formed in this country, and I live in the hope of seeing
you all again, if I shall be spared to revisit the Australian
colonies. (Loud and continued cheering)' (*Sydney Morning
Herald*, 23 Aug 1875).

26 A leading article in the *Sydney Morning Herald* comments,
'There are hundreds of persons in our midst to whom Anthony
Trollope afforded no small amount of both recreation and
instruction, and to whom the great novelist has been for many
years a pleasant companion and a valued friend. Such persons
will cordially sympathize with the desire to do honour to one
who has taken a foremost part in the business of the world's
literature, and will unite in the hope expressed by Sir James
Martin that Mr Trollope's "recollection of us will be only half
as kindly as our recollection of him".'

28 Leaves Sydney aboard the *City of Melbourne* homeward bound
via New Zealand (for one day) and Hawaii. Sleeps on deck
during the voyage: 'I was the only passenger who felt disposed
to make this escape from the cabins.' Arriving at San Francisco
(26 Sep) he is unimpressed. 'There is almost nothing to see in
San Francisco that is worth seeing. . . . There is always a
perfectly cloudless sky overhead, unless when rain is falling
in torrents, and perhaps nowhere in the world is there a more
sudden change from heat to cold on the same day.' Speculation
and commerce are the major concerns of the city, so he visits
the Stock Exchange: 'I thought that the gentlemen employed
were going to hit each other between the eyes, and that
the apparent quarrels which I saw already demanded the
interference of the police.' Visits Yosemite via Merced and
then takes the train across the country, a seven-day journey:
'I never made a journey with less fatigue, less tedium or
less discomfort' (*The Tireless Traveller*, Letter xx, pp. 212–21).
Concludes his tour in Boston and New York. While in Boston
meets Sir George Bowen (1821–99), Governor of Victoria, 1873–
9, then on leave.

September
24 (Fri) Completes *The American Senator* (serialised in *Temple Bar*,
May 1876–July 1877; book publication by Chapman and Hall,
June 1877). [By now reviewers were dwelling on the *rechauffé*
elements in Trollope's fiction while still hankering for the good
old Barchester days. The *Examiner*, focusing on the character

of the husband-hunting Arabella Trefoil, finds AT misanthropic. 'He seems still to keep a special inkstand supplied with gall, for use when describing fashionable society, against which his rancour appears to be unbounded' (21 July 1877, pp. 916–17). By contrast, other notices, particularly that in *The Times*, found the society of Dillsborough done in AT's 'most entertaining manner' (*The Times*, 10 Aug 1877, p. 3).]

October

16 (Sat) AT calls on Longfellow in the afternoon.
20 Sails aboard the *Bothnia* out of New York. Among the passengers is Henry James: 'We had also Anthony Trollope, who wrote novels in his state room all the morning (he does it literally every morning of his life, no matter where he may be), and played cards with Mrs Bronson [Katherine Colman DeKay Bronson (1834–1901), American socialite friend of literary men, including Ruskin and Browning] all the evening. He has a gross and repulsive face and manners, but appears *bon enfant* when you talk with him. But he is the dullest Briton of them all' (*Henry James Letters*, ed. Leon Edel [Cambridge, Mass.] I, 486; II, 94). [James came to admire Trollope and left a fine tribute in 'Anthony Trollope', *Century Magazine*, n.s. IV (July 1883) 385–95, repr. in *Partial Portraits* (1888).]
30 Arrives in Liverpool having completed 33 pages of *An Autobiography* aboard ship. On his return he finds he has been made an honorary freeman of the Grocers' Company.

November

7 (Sun) AT and Harry call on the Leweses. Later AT dines with General R. Taylor and Colonel H. M. Hozier, fellow passengers on the *Bothnia*.
From early this month till mid-December, hunting 'with the fears as to frosts and trembles as to fast bursts; but I think this will be the last of it' (*L*, II, 671).

December

27 (Mon) Declares he has given up smoking.
31 ? Hosts a small male dinner party at which guests include Sir Henry Thompson and perhaps Charles Hall (1843–1900), later Sir Charles, Attorney-General to the Prince of Wales, 1877–92.

1876

January

2 (Sun) Resumes *An Autobiography*.

10 Sends Walter Herries Pollock a wedding present comprising a collection of Elizabethan plays. [Pollock (1850–1926), son of AT's friend and neighbour in Montagu Square Sir Frederick Pollock, Queen's Remembrancer 1874–86, wrote an appreciative article after AT's death in *Harper's New Monthly Magazine*, LXVI (May 1883) 907–12.]

12 Attends a special court of the Grocers' Company to be made an honorary freeman. The citation reads, 'in recognition of the great pleasure afforded to many thousands in their hours of relaxation by his admirable works of fiction; and of the valuable information imparted in the accounts of his travels' (MSS Guildhall Library, cited in *L*, II, 670).

14 ? Charles Hall to dinner.

17 At Lowick, Northamptonshire, home of his friend the Revd W. Lucas Collins, for hunting. He writes to Arthur Sullivan (1842–1900) urging the composer while in Paris to call on Jane Dulany, an amateur singer.

March

2 (Tues) Warmly received when he presents prizes at the second annual meeting of the Quebec Institute, he urges the students to acquire the art of reading now rather than in middle age. Mix light with serious reading, he advises, 'that the one should not engross nor the other weary them'. It is well to be selective about novels but he does not believe that Scott, Thackeray or Dickens 'ever wrote anything impure'.

17 Dines with Sir Thomas Fowell Buxton (1837–1915), MP for King's Lynn 1865–8. Among the guests are John Bright and J. A. Froude.

April

1 (Tues) Completes *An Autobiography*.

30 Deposits manuscript of *An Autobiography* in his desk for Harry (published by Blackwood, Oct 1883). Accompanying the manuscript is a letter: 'I wish you to accept as a gift from me, given you now, the accompanying pages which contain a memoir of my life. My intention is that they shall be published

after my death, and be edited by you. . . . The volume ought to be worth some hundreds of pounds to you' (*L*, II, 685). [Blackwood agreed to pay £1000 for the full copyright of the first 4000 copies and two-thirds of the profits on any additional copies sold (*L*, II, 686).] Decides to give up Essex hunting: 'I am giving away my old horses, and anybody is welcome to my saddles and horse-furniture' (*Auto.*, p. 302).

May
2   (Tues) Begins *The Duke's Children*.
3   Anniversary dinner of Royal Literary Fund with Lord Carnarvon [Henry Howard Molyneux Herbert, 1831–90] in the chair.
6   Attends dinner given by the Lord Mayor of London to honour some 280 representatives of literature. Speakers include J. A. Froude, Sir Francis Doyle, G. A. Sala, Edmund Yates and Tom Taylor (1817–80), editor of *Punch* 1874–80, and popular playwright.
8? Attends House of Lords along with John Blackwood to give evidence before the Royal Commission on Copyright, to which he had been named on 7 April. [The Commission met intermittently for a year, delivering its report on 24 May 1878.]
13 Laid low by a severe bout of influenza.
26 Meeting of the Commission on Copyright.

July
13 (Thurs) Meets Robert Browning and expresses profound dislike of *Deronda* [appearing in monthly parts, 1 Feb–1 Sep 1876]. For comments on *Daniel Deronda*, see *Auto.*, pp. 211–12.
14 Meeting with Octavian Blewitt, Lord Houghton and Sir Frederick Pollock concerning Royal Literary Fund accounts.
At the end of the month, goes abroad with Rose to Felsenegg, four miles from Zug, Switzerland, starting for home late September and arriving mid-October.

October
29 (Sun) Completes *The Duke's Children* (serialised in *All the Year Round*, 4 Oct 1879–14 July 1880; book publication by Chapman and Hall, May 1880). [Strong sympathies were evoked by the trials of the old Duke in a novel judged by the *Spectator* as 'thoroughly readable and one of the most edifying that Mr

Trollope has yet produced', both on the score of its understanding the aristocratic principle and, in more domestic terms, the
relations of parents and children (LIII [12 June 1880] 754–5).
Even the *Saturday Review* had kind words for the main character
(XLIX [12 June 1880] 767–8), while the *Nation*, XXXI (19 Aug
1880) 138–9, called it one of Trollope's most successful novels.
'He is, unless we are greatly mistaken, the last of the realists,
and, like a true Englishman, not even that on any theory. He
paints the world as he sees it, but he sees it with just that
amount of artistic vision which saves his picture from having
the dull flatness of everyday life, and yet never makes the
light and shade any lighter or any darker than everybody feels
to be within the bounds of naturalness.'

November

19   (Sun) ? Dines, accompanied by Florence Bland, with the Friths.
28   With William Powell Frith (1819–1909) dines with Revd William
     Rogers (1819–96), Rector of St Botolph's, Bishopsgate, before
     presenting prizes at the annual meeting of the City and
     Spitalfields School of Art. His topic is 'The Art of Reading'.
     He begins by asking why had he been so invited as one who
     had devoted his life not to the instruction but to the amusement
     of his fellow creatures. His answer is that unless they could
     amuse themselves they could hardly be successful, and he
     recommends them to become readers of good novels. They
     should when still young acquire the reading habit and cultivate
     other pleasures, such as visits to the theatre or the National
     Gallery, where they might view the paintings of his friend
     Frith. The artist recalled of the occasion, 'Trollope made a
     good speech, and I made a bad one' (*My Autobiography and
     Reminiscences* [1887] III, 387).

December

8   (Fri) Speaks at a conference on the Eastern Question in St
     James's Hall. [Public opinion was incensed by the ruthless
     way the Turks had put down popular uprisings in Bulgaria.]
     Thomas Hardy (1840–1928), in the audience, noted, 'Trollope
     outran the five or seven minutes allowed for each speech, and
     the Duke [of Westminster], who was chairman, after various
     soundings of the bell, and other hints that he must stop,
     tugged at Trollope's coat-tails in desperation. Trollope turned

round, exclaimed parenthetically, "Please leave my coat alone", and went on speaking' (Florence Emily Hardy, *The Life of Thomas Hardy, 1840–1928* [1962] pp. 112–13). [AT's speech was reported by the *Pall Mall Gazette*, 8 Dec 1876, p. 8.]

19 ? Adolphus Meetkerke, and his wife, *née* Cecilia Elizabeth Gore (1823?–1903), dine with the Trollopes.

25 ? Kate Field joins the Trollopes for Christmas dinner.

1877

The centrepiece of the year was AT's last major journey, in many ways his most ambitious and taxing, to South Africa. Reading and preparing took up most of June, and he set off at the end of the month, arriving at Cape Town on 22 July. Next day he was at work on the inevitable account of his travels, which took him to the major cities and across vast distances. Rugged terrain and broiling temperatures were not new to him, of course, but he was older now and the strain soon told. He wrote home from Port Elizabeth saying he dreaded some of the journeys facing him: 'Five hundred miles at a stretch, – with four five or six hours allowed at night according to the fancies of the black drivers. However other men get through and I suppose I shall' (*L*, II, 734). As in his travels in Australia, he was constantly bombarded with invitations and speaking engagements, which also took their toll. He met influential figures such as Bishop Colenso, Sir Henry Bulwer and Sir Theophilus Shepstone, and men of business such as George Farrar, who took him over the Diamond Fields. But as always, despite the hardships and homesickness, his optimism and energy saw him through. Arriving in London in January 1878, he wrote exultantly to John Blackwood, 'I have got back alive and well; and as I have survived the passing of various nights in a Boer's best bed, I think I may say that I am qualified to undergo any hardship' (*L*, II, 748).

January

In the middle of the month, Henry James meets AT at the home of Mrs Edward Dicey and finds him 'a very good, genial, ordinary fellow – much better than he seemed on the steamer when I crossed with him' (*Henry James Letters*, ed. Leon Edel [Cambridge, Mass., 1975] II, 94).

26 (Fri) ? Audits accounts of Royal Literary Fund.

February

3 (Sat) Begins *John Caldigate*.

16 ? George Smalley (1833–1916), the American journalist, dines with AT. [Early in their acquaintance Smalley called on him towards noon on one occasion and found the novelist at breakfast. Invited to join him Smalley declined, having breakfasted much earlier. AT roared, 'What . . . do you mean to say you are not man enough to eat two breakfasts?' (*McClure's Magazine*, xx [Jan 1903] 298–9).]

22 Begins work on a biographical study of Cicero.

26 ? Meeting with Edward Dicey.

March

7 (Wed) J. M. Langford relays to John Blackwood a meeting with AT and Sir Henry James, later Lord James of Hereford: 'Trollope raging and roaring with immense vehemence against the system of cross-examination as practised, and James defending it with charming calmness and good nature' (*L*, II, 950).

12 Kate Field's comedy *Extremes Meet* opens at St James's Theatre. AT is an early attender.

15 ? Dines with William Allingham (1824–89), poet, editor of *Fraser's Magazine* 1874–9.

22 ? Dines with Sir Henry Thompson.

April

27 (Fri) Dines with Sir Charles Trevelyan at Grosvenor Crescent. John Bright, also present, finds him 'rather loud and boisterous in his manner of speaking'.

May

9 (Wed) Attends Royal Literary Fund's anniversary dinner, Lord Derby in the chair.

June

4 (Mon) ? Mr and Mrs Austin Dobson dine with the Trollopes.

7 Preparatory to his trip to South Africa, attends lecture

'Thoughts upon the Present and Future of South Africa, and Central and Eastern Africa', delivered at the Royal Colonial Institute by Donald Currie, later Sir Donald (1825–1909), founder of the Castle Steamship Company, MP for Perthshire 1880–5 and West Perthshire 1886–1900. Currie had established a new shipping route between England and Cape Town in 1872.

8   Seeks letters of introduction from Sir Henry Barkly (1815–98), Governor of the Cape Colony for the previous seven years.

9   ? Dines with Donald Currie and meets J. A. Houston (?) the Scottish painter.

20   Nicholas Trübner agrees to pay £175 for 15 travel letters from South Africa. [They appear from October in such newspapers as the *Manchester Examiner and Times*, the Aberdeen *Daily Free Press*, the *Cardiff Times* and the *Preston Guardian*, and are reprinted in the *Cape Times*, 10 Nov 1877–4 Mar 1878 (*L*, II, 732–3).]

23–4   Frances Eleanor Trollope calls to say goodbye on the eve of AT's departure.

29   Embarks from Dartmouth for South Africa on the SS *Caldera*.

July

2   (Mon) Writes to Harry, having got through the Bay of Biscay without disasters, 'I dont like anyone on board, but I hate two persons. There is an old man who plays the flute all the afternoon and evening. I think he and I will have a fight. And there is a beastly impudent young man with a voice like a cracked horn, who will talk to me' (*L*, II, 729).

21   Completes *John Caldigate* (serialised in *Blackwood's*, Apr 1878–June 1879; book publication by Chapman and Hall, May 1879). [Beginning its review with a surprising eulogy for his Irish tales, the *Spectator* saw this Australian novel as similarly powerful and true, calling Hester, the heroine, its great achievement. 'We do not think Mr Trollope has ever drawn so fine, impressive, interesting, and sympathetic a character as this wifeliest of wives and womanliest of women' (LII [19 July 1879] 916–17). Other reviews, less enthusiastic, found the novel rather dull and drawn out.]

22   Arrives at Cape Town. Writes to Frederic Chapman, 'I shall begin my book about South Africa tomorrow!!!' (*L*, II, 730).

23   Begins *South Africa*. Visits Parliament and hears a 'hot debate'

in which John Paterson (1822–80), MP for Port Elizabeth, proved 'the keenest of the wordsmen' (*SA*, i, 94–5).

August

4 (Sat) Sails on the RMS *Natal* for Port Elizabeth.

6 Arriving at Port Elizabeth, finds the population celebrating the birthday of the Duke of Edinburgh, but AT decides the town has a pronounced Yankee flavour.

8 Meets Captain Henry Spalding (1840?–1907) of the Bengal Fusiliers.

10 Arrives in Grahamstown.

14 Dines with the Grahamstown Club. A witness describes AT as appearing 'in a shepherd's plaid, combinations, and, we strongly suspect, a flannel shirt' (*SA*, i, 5). During his tour of the Eastern Province, inspects Heatherton Towers, the leading ostrich farm.

20 At King Williams Town dines with the Town Club.

22 Meets with some 20 chiefs. The spokesman wears 'an old black coat, a flannel shirt, a pair of tweed trousers and a billycock hat, – comfortably and warmly dressed, – with a watch-key of ordinary appearance ingeniously inserted into his ear as an ornament' (*SA*, i, 199–200).

24 Arrives in East London for three days before going on to Durban on the RMS *Stettin*.

29 Arrives in Durban; taken by the Mayor on a trip into Victoria County showing the sugar-growing districts.

September

1 (Sat) Arrives in Pietermaritzburg to stay at the Royal Hotel, but on the invitation of Sir Henry Bulwer (1836–1914), Governor of Natal 1875–80, he moves to Government House.

2 Hears Bishop Colenso preach [John William Colenso (1814–83), Bishop of Natal].

5 Anticipating a visit from AT, Frank Colenso, the Bishop's son, notes, 'We are almost afraid lest he should fall completely into the hands of the officials and be hoodwinked. And yet, I imagine, he will prove too keen an observer for them to deceive him. It will be a great triumph if we can supply him with really trustworthy facts about Zululand' (Frances Sarah Colenso, *Letters from Natal*, ed. Wyn Rees [Pietermaritzburg, 1958] pp. 337–8).

6 Public banquet given by the Mayor. A Natal journal observed representation of 'every imaginable interest contained within the boundaries of the colony' (*SA*, i, 6–7). AT makes a speech which is warmly applauded.

8–11 Joins Bulwer on viceregal tour of upland sugar districts, entering houses of Germans, Hollanders, Boers and colonial English. Bulwer finds AT 'a cheery, good-natured hearty man' (*SA*, i, 8).

13 Leaves for the Transvaal. Travelling by post-cart for two and a half days, he reaches Newcastle, joining up with George Herbert Farrar (1859–1915), later Sir George, businessman, member of the Transvaal Legislative Council, for a tour of the Diamond Fields. [For an account of this journey see *SA*, Appendix C, pp. 474–87.]

18 Travelling at 30 miles a day, the party takes a week to reach Pretoria.

24 Conducted to Government House, guest of Sir Theophilus Shepstone (1817–93) [Secretary of Native Affairs for Natal 1856–76; administrator of the Transvaal 1877–9; effected annexation of the Transvaal in 1877]. During the stay at Government House, meets a young member of Shepstone's staff, Henry Rider Haggard (1856–1925), later Sir Henry, popular novelist. Rider Haggard noted, 'I talked with him a good deal, he has the most peculiar ideas and is as obstinate as a pig' (Lilias Rider Haggard, *The Cloak that I Left: A Biography of the Author, Henry Rider Haggard, KBE* [1951] p. 73).

October

1 (Mon) In company with Farrar sets out for the Diamond Fields. Severe drought causes problems with horses.

7 Writes from the Transvaal to Harry, 'I do so long to get home. South Africa is so dirty' (*L*, ii, 740). Reports on slow progress of 35 miles a day and losing one horse to cholera.

9 At Mossel Bay, a resort between Cape Town and Port Elizabeth.

12 Entering Kimberley, AT discovers that the trunk containing his manuscript for the travel book on South Africa has been lost. After much anxiety the trunk is recovered. Stays at Government House with Major Owen (later Sir Owen) Lanyon (1842–87), known from earlier days in Ireland. Lanyon was appointed Administrator of Griqualand West in 1875 after a military career in the West Indies and West Africa.

15 Writes to Harry, 'I have been handling diamonds till I am sick of them' (*L*, II, 742).
22 Leaves Kimberley for Bloemfontein accompanied by Lanyon. Stays at Free State Hotel. During his visit meets J. H. Brand (1823–88), later Sir John, President of the Orange Free State.

November
 8 (Thurs) After visiting Thaba 'Nchu and Grahamstown, leaves Port Elizabeth for Mossel Bay, where Resident Magistrate George Hudson shows him grand scenery. AT writes to Harry next day, 'The grandest scenery in the world to me would be Montagu Square' (*L*, II, 740).
9–17 Visits George, Knysna and Oudtshoorn, inspecting the Cango Caves. Leaves for Cape Town on RMS *Dublin Castle*.
18 Arrives at Cape Town and stays at the leading hotel, Rathfelder's. During his visit accompanies Thomas E. Fuller (1831–1910), manager of the Union Steamship Co., on a tour of wine-growing districts.

December
 1 (Sat) At Geres in the wine district.
11 Leaves Cape Town for home aboard RMS *Nubian*, arriving in England on 3 January 1878.

1878

January
 2 (Wed) Completes *South Africa* (published by Chapman and Hall, Feb 1878).
 3 Arrives in London.
11 Blackwood welcomes him back: 'No one . . . can rough it better than our Mail clad Anthony' (*L*, II, 749).
25 Recovering from a severe bout of influenza. 'I wish myself back in South Africa' (*L*, II, 754).
30 Advises Squire Bancroft (1841–1926), later Sir Squire, actor and manager, on mode of election to the Athenaeum: 'The selected heroes are generally learned pundits, philosophers, doctors who have invented new diseases, and scientific fogies with bleared eyes' (*L*, II, 755).

February
3 (Sun) At Highclere, Hampshire, seat of Lord Carnarvon, former Colonial Secretary.
7 Dines at Sir Henry Thompson's with GHL, Alma-Tadema, R. F. Burton, the critic J. Cordy Jeaffreson (1831–1901), Leslie Stephen and Sir Frederick Pollock.
18 Dines with Escott at the Thatched House Club, St James's. Also present are Col. Colley (Lord Lytton's private secretary), J. A. Froude, Major Arthur Griffiths, Dr. R. Quain, J. C. Parkinson and Edmund Yates. AT tells the company of his relations with official authority at the Post Office. [For a story concerning Frederic Hill see *I & R*, pp. 53–4. Hill (1803–1906), brother of Rowland, was Assistant Secretary of the Post Office, 1851–75.]
24 Entertains John Blackwood to dinner. Blackwood relates to his nephew William the next day, 'We had a cheery dinner at the Trollopes' yesterday. Anthony has come back [from South Africa] in great force. Lord John [Manners] says he is like to drive them all mad at the weary Copyright Commission, going over all the ground that has been discussed in his absence' (Porter, *Annals of a Publishing House*, p. 317).

March
Early this month, active soliciting subscriptions for a marble bust of Thackeray. At around the same time, disposes of his horses.
1 (Fri) ? At the Garrick with Lord Barrington (1824–86), MP for Eye, Suffolk, 1866–80, and Lord Stanley.
2 Robert Buchanan (1841–1901) commissions a story for his periodical, *Light*. AT obliges with 'The Lady of Launay'.
13 Learning of the engagement of George Smith's eldest daughter, Elizabeth, AT offers her some advice: 'How you must find out what he likes best to eat, – and never let him have it lest it should disagree. How you must remember always to sit up for him if he should ever go to the club. How you should always have your own way about everything inside the house because you are a woman, and take care that he never has his outside the house because he might go astray as a man' (*L*, II, 762).
Late this month, heavily involved in arrangements for the Royal Literary Fund dinner, AT enlists among the stewards Matthew Arnold, A. W. Kinglake, Millais, Reade, Dicey, Baron Emly, and

other lords – 48 Stewards in all. Arthur Penrhyn Stanley (1815–81), Dean of Westminster, takes the chair.

April

23 (Tues) At Bolton Bridge, remaining until 2 May.
25 Begins *Ayala's Angel*.

May

9 (Thurs) ? The Trollopes entertain Anne Procter (1799–1888), widow of the poet Bryan Waller Procter ('Barry Cornwall').
31 Guest of George Joachim Goschen (1831–1907), later Viscount Goschen, to meet the Princess Royal (Queen Victoria's eldest daughter) and her husband, the Crown Prince of Germany. Also present are GE and GHL, by special request of the Princess Royal. '22 at dinner and a number of swells and celebrities afterwards' (*GE*, vii, 28).

June

22 (Sat) Travels to Iceland in yacht *Mastiff*; writes *How the 'Mastiffs' Went to Iceland* (privately printed, October 1878). Returns home on 8 July.

July

11 (Thurs) Guest of honour at prize-giving of Margate High School on invitation of Mrs Ellen Robinson [*née* Ellen Ternan (1839–1914), sister of TAT's second wife and Dickens' mistress]. One of AT's grandsons eventually attended the school. In his speech AT comments, 'I went to school when I was seven, and I left school when I was nineteen, and in all those years I don't think I ever saw a prize, and I'm sure I never got one!' (*L*, ii, 780).
24 Goes abroad to Switzerland and Germany until 30 September with Rose and Florence Bland. Writing to GE from Felsenegg (13 Aug) he refers to his routine: 'Here we are on the top of a mountain, where I write for four hours a day, walk for four hours, eat for two, and sleep out the balance satisfactorily' (*L*, ii, 785).

September

24 (Tues) Completes *Ayala's Angel* (published by Chapman and Hall, May 1881). [Most reviews agreed that, while the plot was negligible, Ayala was a fascinating character. The story,

said the *Illustrated London News*, LXXVIII (28 May 1881) 526, 'has
the singular charm of undeniable reality, as regards the
sayings, and doings, and correspondences of the various
personages'.]

26 Writing to G. W. Rusden from Freiburg-im-Breisgau, AT
    announces he has just completed his eightieth tale: 'I doubt
    whether a greater mass of prose fiction ever came from one
    pen' (*L*, II, 792).

October
26 (Sat) Begins *Cousin Henry*.

November
11 (Mon) ? Millais to dine.
14? Attends semi-public dinner with the Mayor of Manchester.
15 At Manchester Athenaeum, delivers his lecture 'The Native
    Races of South Africa'. Accepts a dinner invitation prior to the
    lecture from Alexander Ireland (1810–94), manager of the
    Manchester Examiner and Times 1846–86, with a cautionary
    note warning, 'Too liberal a bowl is not good for lecturing'
    (*L*, II, 800).
30 Death of GHL.

December
4   (Wed) AT attends GHL's funeral at Highgate Cemetery.
8   Charles Lewes calls inviting AT to write a short memoir of his
    father. Completes *Cousin Henry* (serialised simultaneously in
    the *Manchester Weekly Times* and *North British Weekly Mail*, 8
    Mar–24 May 1879; book publication by Chapman and Hall,
    Oct 1879). [The general theme of criticism was how Trollope
    could make interesting the trite subject matter of lost wills and
    legacy hunters. That he could and did in novel after novel
    haunted reviewers. The *Examiner* decided that in this case it
    was the operation of Henry's mind under temptation that kept
    the story alive (25 Oct 1879, p. 1382). For the critic writing in
    the *Spectator*, LII (18 Oct 1879) 1319–21, the secret of Trollope's
    handling of familiar sensational materials was his admirably
    paced and unemotional narration. 'His touch is eminently
    civilizing; everything, from the episodes to the sentences,
    moves without hitch or creak; we never have to read a
    paragraph twice, and we are never sorry to have read it
    once.']
23 Begins *Marion Fay* (breaks off after nine days).

1879

In his last years Trollope remained very active. Reading, always a solace (*Auto.*, p. 315) – instead of hunting – became a passion. Between 1866 and 1882 AT read more than 270 plays ['Anthony Trollope's Notes on the Old Drama', ed. Elizabeth Epperley, forthcoming, *English Literary Studies*, British Columbia, Victoria]. His clubs, the Garrick and the Athenaeum, still drew him for afternoon whist and conversation. And, as always, novels flowed from his unstoppable pen, or, more frequently now, were dictated to his devoted niece, Florence Bland. In October 1876 he had written to G. W. Rusden emphatically, 'No, I certainly do not like idleness' (*L*, II, 696). In summer 1880 he left Montagu Square, where he had enjoyed the past seven years, for the more tranquil countryside of Harting, on the Sussex–Hampshire border, near Petersfield. With characteristic spirit he set to work: 'I am as busy as would be one thirty years younger, in cutting out dead boughs, and putting a paling here and a little gate there' (*L*, II, 887–8). His last years, Cecilia Meetkerke justly observed, were 'still full of profit and pleasure' and 'the punctual and deliberate habits of years were only slightly modified'. The local parson recalled Trollope riding in the parish, attending school management meetings, promoting lectures, and attending Holy Communion, 'an alert and reverend and audible worshipper' – unquestionably the last. He virtually died in harness. Although warned of angina, he stubbornly insisted on travelling to Ireland to gather material for *The Landleaguers*. But the clamorous and indefatigable Trollope collapsed in an appropriately robust fashion, roaring with laughter among friends listening to a popular novel being read aloud.

January
8   (Wed) Meeting of the Royal Literary Fund Committee.

February
1   (Sat) Begins *Thackeray*. He seeks information from Lady Ritchie (Anne Thackeray) and Edward Fitzgerald [see under 25 Feb]. AT quails before his task: 'There is absolutely nothing to say, – except washed out criticism. But it had to be done, and no one would do it so lovingly' (*L*, II, 815).
    Pays tribute to GHL in *Fortnightly Review*: 'There was never a man so pleasant as he with whom to sit and talk vague

literary gossip over a cup of coffee and a cigar' ('GHL', n.s.
xxv, 15–24).
12   Meeting of Royal Literary Fund Committee. ? Dinner guest is
      (?Sir Henry) Thompson.
15   ? Dines at the Garrick with American author Bret Harte (1836–
      1902).
20   ? Dines with General Sir Charles and Lady Trollope.
25   Edward Fitzgerald writes to Frederick Tennyson, 'Trollope
      (Anthony) wrote to me for particulars of Thackeray between
      1833–40 being engaged to make a sort of Biography of WMT
      for Macmillan. . . . I am glad Trollope has the job if to be
      done at all: he is a Gentleman as well as an Author – was a
      loyal friend of Thackeray's, and so, I hope, will take him out
      of any Cockney Worshipper's hands' (*The Letters of Edward
      Fitzgerald*, ed. A. M. and A. B. Terhune, IV, 182–3).

March
25   (Tues) Completes *Thackeray* (published by Macmillan, May
      1879).

April
 3   (Thurs) William Blackwood (1836–1912), nephew of John Black-
      wood, calls regarding reissue of *Nina Balatka* and *Linda Tressel*.
      AT is elected to the council of the Metropolitan Free Libraries
      Association, a body dedicated to adoption of the Public Free
      Library Act calling for a penny levy on the rates for providing
      free libraries, heartily resisted in some quarters. Thomas
      Hughes is among the supporting speakers. [AT presides over
      two meetings, 27 May and 18 June.]
 8   Begins *Dr Wortle's School*, at Lowick Rectory, Northampton-
      shire, home of the Revd W. Lucas Collins: 'That I, who have
      belittled so many clergymen, should ever come to live in a
      parsonage!' (*L*, II, 822).
29   Completes *Dr Wortle's School* (serialised in *Blackwood's*, May–
      Dec 1880; book publication by Chapman and Hall, Jan 1881).
      [In general, the journals found the novel brisk and bracing,
      with lively characterisation. The *Westminster Review* declared
      that the characters were endowed 'with a true vitality, with a
      distinct reality, which compels us to follow their fortunes with
      interest' (CXVI [July 1881] 283–4). The scenes at Chicago were

recommended by the American journal *Nation*, with praise for 'an antique flavour which carries one back to days of *Martin Chuzzlewit*' (XXXII [10 Mar 1881] 172–3).]

May
21 (Wed) Visits GE, who has recently suffered 'a severe attack of pain', and stays with her an hour.

June
15 (Sun) Organises a dinner party, inviting Lord Aberdare and Thomas Hughes to discuss the Free Libraries.

July
Possibly this month, tea with Mrs Anne Proctor and Henry Adams (1838–1918), distinguished historian and editor of the *North American Review*, who later described AT as 'a rosy-gilled John Bull'.
8 (Tues) Hard at work all day at the new house, the Trollopes take a break in Petersfield.
10 Between now and 7 September, publishes 11 articles appearing at intervals in the *Pall Mall Gazette*. [The articles were collected by Michael Sadleir as *London Tradesmen* (1927).]
17 Rose leaves for the continent.
23 ? Dines at the Garrick with Millais.

August
1 (Fri) Goes abroad to meet Rose and Florence Bland. They travel to the Vosges (France), Felsenegg (Switzerland) and the Black Forest (Germany). During August AT goes to Baden to visit TAT, who is suffering from sciatica. Returns home on 30 September.
6 Resumes *Marion Fay*.

October
18 (Sat) The *Pall Mall Gazette* deals harshly with *Thackeray*. A reference in it to Thackeray's finances occasions a coolness between AT and Anne, Thackeray's daughter.
23 Gives lecture, 'The Zulus and Zululand', at Nottingham.
28 Gives lecture, 'The Condition of the Zulu People', at the Harborne and Edgbaston Institute, Birmingham.

November

21   (Fri) Completes *Marion Fay* (serialised in the *Graphic*, 3 Dec
      1881–3 June 1882; book publication by Chapman and Hall,
      May 1882). [The novel's familiar Trollopian blend of love and
      pathos brought favourable notices, but it was generally agreed
      that the issues of marriage across class boundaries had been
      avoided.]

24   Back in London, arranges meeting with Sir Charles Trollope.

December

11   (Thurs) Meets Sir Frederick Leighton (1830–96), distinguished
      artist, who declines an invitation to take the chair at the Royal
      Literary Fund anniversary dinner. AT proceeds to invite Millais
      to perform the task.

(Mid-month)   Calls on Georgiana Hogarth (1827–1917), younger
sister of Dickens' wife, Catherine, and leaves his card.

20   ? Breakfast visit from Mary Elizabeth Christie.

21   Writes to Harry, 'I miss you most painfully. But I had
      expected that. I only hope that you may come back with the
      summer. . . . Nothing really frightens me but the idea of
      enforced idleness. As long as I can write books, even though
      they be not published, I think that I can be happy' (*L*, ii, 886).

Late this year, Julian Hawthorne (1846–1934) meets AT at a social
gathering given by an 'eminent publisher', possibly Chapman and
Hall. He finds 'a broad-shouldered, sturdy man, of middle height,
with a ruddy countenance, and snow-white tempestuous beard
and hair. He wore large, gold-rimmed spectacles, but his eyes
were black and brilliant, and looked at his interlocutor with a
certain genial fury of inspection' (*Confessions and Criticisms* [Boston,
Mass., 1887] p. 140).

1880

January

21   (Wed) ? Audit of Royal Literary Fund accounts.

27   ? Directors' meeting of Chapman and Hall. [As one of the
      three directors of Chapman and Hall, since it had become a
      limited company, AT was engaged twice a week with lengthy
      meetings which he found inconvenient and disagreeable

demands on his time. He was further troubled by the decision
to leave his Montagu Square house and move to the country.]

May

1 (Sat) Attends banquet of the Royal Academy at which Gladstone is present. Next day writes to the Prime Minister to
inquire if he has in any way offended him. Gladstone's
response is to allay such apprehensions, blaming himself for
any misunderstandings 'due only to the absorption of the
present times' [Gladstone had just formed his second
ministry].

26 Completes *The Life of Cicero* (published by Chapman and Hall,
late Nov 1880).

June

24 (Thurs) Discusses with Frederic Chapman (?) publication by
Dickens and Evans of Harry's book on sociology.

July

6 (Tues) Gives up 39 Montagu Square and settles at North End,
South Harting, Sussex.

23 Arranging his large library, AT complains to Harry of lack of
shelf space. He is also busy with iron bins for his wine. He
begins to look about him: 'We have two horses, and a
brougham, and a pony carriage. The pony is a nice little beast
but rather old. We like the neighbours as far as we have seen
them as yet' (*L*, II, 877).

29 Being so occupied with the move to Harting, he forgets his
responsibility as one of the auditors of the Royal Literary
Fund.

August

3 (Tues) ? Meeting with Frederic Chapman.

16 Marriage of AT's niece, 'Bice', to Charles Beilby Stuart-Wortley
(1851–1926), later Lord Stuart of Wortley.

18 Begins *Kept in the Dark*.

October

13 (Wed) Attends Gaudy at New College, Oxford.

16 ? Stays with John Tilley at 73 St George's Square.

17   In London for a few days. ? Dines with George Smalley at the Garrick.
21   ? Dinner with George Smalley at the Garrick.
24   ? Dinner with Sir Charles and Lady Trollope.

November
29   (Mon) Presents copies of *The Life of Cicero* to the Athenaeum.

December
15   (Wed) Completes *Kept in the Dark* (serialised in *Good Words*, May–Dec 1882; book publication by Chatto and Windus, Oct 1882). [Some reviews appeared soon after AT's death and the novel was accordingly treated with decent respect. Tributes such as that of the *British Quarterly Review*, LXXVII (Jan 1883) 220–1, were typical: 'In him our lighter literature has lost a man of distinctive gifts, whose place in it has not only been large but distinguished.']
17   Begins *The Fixed Period*.
24   Deeply moved by GE's death (on the 22nd).

1881

January
24   (Mon) Snowbound in the country, AT chafes at inactivity.

February
28   (Thurs) Completes *The Fixed Period* (serialised in *Blackwood's*, Oct 1881–Mar 1882; book publication by Blackwood, Mar 1882). [AT's one attempt at a futuristic novel seems to have puzzled reviewers, although most were inclined to label it a rather heavy-handed *jeu d'esprit*.]

March
2   (Wed) ? Board meeting of Chapman and Hall.
5   Goes to Rome and Florence with Rose and Florence Bland. By chance meets Mrs Oliphant in Florence. Returns home on 6 May.
14   Begins *Mr Scarborough's Family*.
29   Meets E. A. Freeman for the first time in Rome. Their

dispute in 1869 over field sports is forgotten as they explore the site of Tusculum and exchange classical anecdotes: 'Mr Trollope was quite willing to hear me talk about Mamilius, and I was more than willing to hear Mr Trollope talk about Cicero. That was a subject on which he talked well and wisely, both on that day and other times' ('Anthony Trollope', *Macmillan's Magazine*, xlvii [Jan 1883] 236–40).

May
17 (Tues) Dines at Millais's with all-male company, including Hardy, Sir Henry Thompson and the composer Arthur Sullivan, who wins £6 from AT at cards.

June
25 (Sat) Florence Bland is convalescing after a severe illness. AT is suffering from heart trouble but continues regular trips to London.

July
3 (Sun) ? Dines with Millais.

August
Possibly this month, elected to United Service Club.
10 The Vardys, particular friends of Rose, visit Harting, staying till the 15th.
29 AT is urged by Henry Howard (1826–1905), a former Governor of Rhode Island, to bring back some old favourites of the Barchester novels. With some reluctance he writes 'The Two Heroines of Plumplington'.

September
15 (Thurs) At Capethorne, Cheshire, home of William Bromley Davenport (1822–84), MP for North Warwickshire 1864–84.
20 Visits Winchester with the Tilleys.
28–9 In London, calls at the Athenaeum.

October
21 (Fri) At the Garrick.
31 Completes *Mr Scarborough's Family* (serialised in *All the Year Round*, 27 May 1882–16 June 1883; book publication by Chatto and Windus, Apr 1883). [The singular character at the heart

of this novel was appreciated by a few critics as something out of the ordinary, although not worked out fully. William Wallace in the *Academy*, xxiii (19 May 1883) 344, pronounced it 'a very enjoyable novel'; the *Saturday Review*, lv (19 May 1883) 642, declared that an 'abundance of "go"' was not enough to redeem it; the *Westminster Review*, cxx (July 1883) 301, praised 'remarkable studies of character' and ingenious plot.]

November
Possibly this month, begins *Lord Palmerston*.
23   (Wed) In London for the Royal Literary Fund.

December
Why Frau Frohmann Raised her Prices is published by William Isbister (?1838–1916), former partner with Strahan and Co.
30   (Fri) ? Guests at Harting include J. M. Langford, Blackwood's London manager, and Henry Richard Tedder (1850–1924), President of the Library Association.

1882

January
15   (Sun) Increasingly troubled by asthma, hernia and heart trouble, AT has been examined by Dr William Murrell (1853–1912), an authority on heart disease: 'He says that I have not a symtom [*sic*] of A.P. [angina pectoris] and that Cross [Robert Schackleford Cross, his local physician] is an old idiot. I am disposed to believe him. Therefore I am going at once to walk up all the hills in the country' (*L*, ii, 939).
26   ? Dines with Lady Trollope.
27   ? Dines with Sir Henry Thompson while in London for a few engagements.

February
Possibly this month, calls on Lady Ritchie and they make up their quarrel: 'I never saw dear Mr Trollope again' (Winifred Gerin, *Anne Thackeray Ritchie: A Biography* [1981] p. 193).
1   (Wed) Completes *Palmerston* (published by Isbister, June 1882).
1–3   Again in London.
7   Engages in some judicious lobbying on behalf of Harry, who

is seeking election to the Athenaeum. He gets in on the 13th by a large vote.
19 Writes to Harry, 'I am thinking of taking a run over to Ireland in reference to a book I am thinking of writing [*The Landleaguers*]' (*L*, II, 950).
20 Begins *An Old Man's Love*.

March
4 (Sat) Back in London. ? Breakfasts with William Blackwood.
11–17 In London. [His usual custom is to stay at Garlants Hotel, Pall Mall, move around his clubs, notably the Garrick and the Athenaeum, and dine with his wide circle of friends. One such arrangement involved a joke by John Tilley's children, John and Edith. AT had invited himself to lunch saying he needed only a crust and some cheese. When he arrived he was led into a back room where they had set out 'the tail end of a stale loaf, some mouldy bits of cheese, and a jug of water'. AT looked with loathing at the table, and Edith told him if he had changed his mind there was lunch in the dining room, at which 'he fairly roared and hugged her like a bear' – Sir John Tilley, *London to Tokyo* (1942) p. 8.]
13 Meeting of Chapman and Hall board.
22 Undergoing examinations by his doctors.

April
4–5 (Tues–Wed) In London. ? Dines with Charles Stuart-Wortley at the Garrick. ? Meets with William Isbister.
20–1 In London. ? Interview with Isbister. Medical check-up by Dr Murrell.

May
9 (Tues) Completes *An Old Man's Love* (published by Blackwood, Mar 1884). [Appearing after *The Landleaguers* helped this novel, allowing reviewers to describe it as a more finished performance. *The Times* commented that 'he needed elbow-room for the effective display of his powers', but conceded that this short tale was 'unusually compact and complete' (14 Apr 1884, p. 3). The *Saturday Review* decided it was 'not an unfitting finale to an almost unparalleled series of works in fiction' (LVII [29 Mar 1884] 414–15).]
15 Travels to Ireland with Florence Bland on the first of two exhausting journeys to collect material for *The Landleaguers*.

[This was a hazardous undertaking for a man in precarious health, and it was politically dangerous. Agitation was rife among the Land League. Lord Frederick Cavendish (1836–82), Chief Secretary for Ireland, was murdered in Phoenix Park, Dublin, 6 May.] Returns home on 13 June.

18　At Dublin, dines with G. C. Cornwall, Secretary of Dublin Post Office.

19　At Cork, calls on Judge John O'Hagan (1822–90), judge in the High Court of Justice 1881–90, and John Edward Vernon (1816–87), director of the Bank of Ireland.

20　Breakfasts with an Irish land-law judge at Cork, and dines with him the following day.

22　To Dunmanway Court, Co. Cork.

23　To Limerick, where he is taken on a tour by Charles Dalton Clifford Lloyd (1844–91), Resident Magistrate for Co. Down 1874–81, Special Resident Magistrate at Kilmallock, Co. Limerick, 1881–3. AT writes reassuringly to Rose that he is safe.

26　Four miles from Clonmel, where he visits slate quarries.

27　Returns to Limerick and proceeds to Galway after a few days.

June

Begins *The Landleaguers*.

1　(Thurs) At Recess, Co. Galway, enjoying a brief holiday from 'Irish difficulties and Irish rebels'. With Florence Bland, visits Connemara.

4　At Westport, Co. Mayo.

7–8　In Dublin.

13　? Calls on John Dicks.

July

22　(Sat) Dines at Lincoln's Inn Fields with Escott.

31　TAT and Frances Eleanor Trollope arrive for a visit at Harting, staying until 9 August.

August

11　(Fri) Returns to Ireland (till 11 Sep) to collect more material.

14–16　At Glendalough, Co. Wicklow, severely pained by asthma attacks.

18–21　At Wooden Bridge, Co. Wicklow, dines with Sir Charles Booth (1812–96).

23　Stays a night with Sir Charles Stanley Monck (1819–94).

27–8 Guest of Lord and Lady Carysfort of County Wicklow, before travelling to Kingstown for a week.

September

2 (Sat) Resumes *The Landleaguers* (left incomplete; serialised in *Life*, 16 Nov 1882–4 Oct 1883; book publication by Chatto and Windus, Oct 1883). [As an unfinished work and one dealing with a vexed political question of Irish unrest the book found little favour, the *Spectator* calling it 'a long pamphlet, under the guise of fiction' (LVI [15 Dec 1883] 1627).]

29 Greatly excited at the imminent arrival of Harry, arranges rooms at Garlants Hotel from 2 October.

October

10 (Tues) Another session with his heart specialist Dr Murrell.

11 ? Meeting with Frederic Chapman. ? Dinner with John Patten Good, a former Post Office colleague.

23 Suffering from his asthma, AT administers some chloral so that he can rest. [At this time he is searching for rooms in the Piccadilly and Victoria areas, because the damp climate at Harting disagrees with him.] Despite his physical condition, he has accepted E. A. Freeman's invitation to visit him at Somerlease, near Wells, Somerset.

25 Travels to Somerset, where he stays until the 27th. Freeman wrote of the visit that the novelist joined him and the Bishop of Clifton in a ramble around Wells 'that he might look out on the land of Barset, if Barset it was to be'. On the 26th the party rambled in Wells and Glastonbury, and argument erupted as to the source of Barchester. 'Barset was Somerset', AT insisted, 'but Barchester was Winchester, not Wells' (*Macmillan's Magazine*, Jan 1883, pp. 236–40).

27 AT has received an asthma remedy from Cardinal Newman (1801–90).

November

1 (Wed) Dinner at the Garrick with Robert Browning, who noted, 'He was taken ill the day after the dinner, – and died some weeks after' (*L*, II, 989). [AT suffered his stroke two days later in fact.]

2 Dines with the Macmillans at Tooting along with Freeman. 'He talked as well and heartily as usual. . . . there was nothing

to put it into anyone's head that the end was so near. The next day came his seizure, and from that day onwards the newspapers told his tale.' [*The Times* published 13 bulletins on his condition.]

3   Suffers a stroke which results in paralysis of the right side accompanied by loss of speech. Harry telegraphs TAT in Rome. [During the next few weeks Sir Richard Quain (1816–98), long-time friend and physician, and Sir William Jenner (1815–98), Physician in Ordinary to the Queen, attend the case. Sir John Tilley, then a child at boarding school, was given an account of the collapse: 'after dinner my sister read *Vice Versa* aloud to him and my father, also a great laugher. Uncle Tony roared as usual; suddenly my father and sister noticed that while they were laughing he was silent: he had had a stroke from which he never recovered' (Tilley, *London to Tokyo*, p. 8).]

December

5   (Tues) Millais writes to Russell, 'I regret to say that dear old Trollope is in a *very critical state*, and I believe there is little hope. I have called frequently and know that he is rarely conscious and has only been able to utter one word since the attack – "No." . . . Need I say more to prove how hopeless his condition is, and is there one word necessary from me to say what I think of the man we have both lost? "Fill up the ranks and march on" – as Dickens said when he heard of Thackeray's death – is the spirit in which I pass on to other subjects' (J. B. Atkins, *The Life of Sir William Howard Russell* [1911] II, 316–17).

6   Dies in a nursing home at 34 Welbeck Street.

7   TAT writes from Rome, 'The last time I saw him was when I went up to his bedroom at Garlants in the morning before we started for Dover. But what will most remain in mind will be the pleasant strolling up and down in the orchard at Harting as we watched and laughed at the dog jumping for the apples! For more than sixty years we have loved each other well; and, as I believe, we shall meet again' (*L*, II, 1037).

9   AT is buried in Kensal Green. Among the mourners are Robert Browning, J. E. Millais, Alfred Austin, Frederic Chapman and G. W. Rusden.

Appendix A
Trollope's Lectures and Speeches, 1861–79

Date	Subject/occasion	Place
4 Jan 1861	'The Civil Service as a Profession', for Post Office Library and Literary Association	St Martin's le Grand, London
15 May 1861	Royal Literary Fund anniversary dinner; responds to toast 'The Literature of England' coupled with the name of Mr Anthony Trollope	Freemasons' Hall, Great Queen Street, London
11 June 1862	Alpine Club; responds to welcome as guest	The Castle, Richmond
30 Dec 1862	'The Present Condition of the Northern States of the American Union'	? Midlands
13 Jan 1863	ditto	? London
13 May 1863	Royal Literary Fund anniversary dinner; responds to toast 'The Writers of Fiction'	Willis's Rooms, London
26? Jan 1864	'Politics as a Daily Study for Common People'	Bury St Edmunds
18 Feb 1864	ditto, for Leeds Mechanics' Institution and Literary Society	Institute Hall, Leeds

Date	Subject/occasion	Place
25 Feb 1864	'On American Affairs', for Halstead Literary and Mechanics' Institute	Halstead Town Hall
? 8 Apr 1864	? Lecture [Source: Princeton notebooks. I have found no further trace]	Tottenham
11 May 1864	With Dickens in the chair, AT speaks at meeting in favour of Shakespeare Foundation Schools in connection with Royal Dramatic College	New Adelphi Theatre, London
18 May 1864	Royal Literary Fund anniversary dinner; AT responds to toast 'Prosperity to English Literature, and the Health of Mr Anthony Trollope'	St James's Hall, London
9 Feb 1866	Farewell speech to William Bokenham on his retirement as Controller of the Circulation Office in the Post Office. Next day's *Times* calls AT's speech 'admirable'	London Coffee House, Ludgate Hill

Date	*Subject/occasion*	*Place*
2 May 1866	Royal Literary Fund anniversary dinner; AT gives toast 'The Pioneers of Civilisation' coupled with the names of Viscount Milton and Sir Samuel Baker	Willis's Rooms
1867	'The Higher Education of Women'. Parrish surmised (*Four Lectures*, p. 67) that the lecture was given in several places. Blank spaces in the text allowed AT to substitute the name of the town he was in. I have not been able to trace any dates for this lecture. But see *L*, i, 377, and ii, 633, the latter clearly relating to this lecture, probably given in early Nov 1874	
4 May 1867	Royal Academy annual dinner; AT responds to toast 'The Interests of Literature'	Royal Academy, London
15 May 1867	Royal Literary Fund anniversary dinner; responds to toast 'Imaginative Literature and Mr Anthony Trollope'	Willis's Rooms

Date	Subject/occasion	Place
31 Oct 1867	Returns thanks for toast to his health at farewell dinner to mark his resignation from the Post Office	Albion Tavern, London
2 Nov 1867	Dickens' farewell; AT responds to toast to literature	Freemasons' Hall
? 18 Mar 1868	? Lecture to students by invitation of the Revd William Rogers	Bishopsgate Institute, London
Oct/Nov 1868	Campaign speeches in Beverley in his bid for election as MP	
10 Apr 1869	Dickens' banquet; AT speaks for light literature	St George's Hall, Liverpool
5 May 1869	Royal Literary Fund anniversary dinner; AT responds to toast to English literature	Willis's Rooms
20–8 Jan 1870	'On English Prose Fiction as a Rational Amusement'	Hull, Glasgow, Edinburgh
31 Jan 1870	ditto	Birmingham
17 Jan 1871	'On English Prose Fiction'	Leeds Philosophical and Literary Society
19 Jan 1871	ditto, for Walsall Lecture Institute	Walsall Temperance Hall

Date	Subject/occasion	Place
20 Jan 1871	'On English Prose Fiction'	Stourbridge, Worcestershire
29 Apr 1871	Royal Academy annual dinner; responds to toast 'The Interests of Literature'	Royal Academy
17 May 1871	Royal Literary Fund anniversary dinner; responds to toast to literature	Freemasons' Hall
Oct 1871–Oct 1872	Numerous speaking engagements at receptions, banquets, etc., during tour of Australia and New Zealand	
18 Dec 1871	'On English Prose Fiction'	Yorick Club, Melbourne
1 Feb 1872	'Modern English Fiction as a Recreation for Young People'	Hobart, Tasmania
13 Nov 1873	Prize-giving for students of Liverpool Institute; speaks on 'The Teaching of Novels'	Institute Hall, Liverpool
Early Nov 1874	? 'The Higher Education of Women'	?
May–Aug 1875	Numerous speaking engagements during second visit to Australia	

Date	Subject/occasion	Place
18 May 1875	Speech at launching of New Guinea Scientific Expedition	Sydney
21 Aug 1875	Response to tribute by Chief Justice of New South Wales, Sir James Martin	Sydney
2 Mar 1876	Prize-giving at 2nd annual meeting of the Quebec Institute; AT speaks on importance of reading novels	Quebec Institute, London
28 Nov 1876	Prize-giving at City and Spitalfields School of Art; AT speaks on 'The Art of Reading'	City and Spitalfields School of Art, London
8 Dec 1876	Conference on the Eastern Question, chaired by the Duke of Westminster; AT contributes a speech	St James's Hall
7 June 1877	Speaks in support of J. A. Froude's plan on safeguards for Zulu people in the Transvaal	Royal Colonial Institute, London
14 Jan 1878	On South Africa	Royal Geographical Society, London
11 July 1878	Prize-giving at Margate High School; AT speaks as guest of honour	Margate High School, Kent
15 Nov 1878	'The Native Races of South Africa'	Manchester Athenaeum

Date	Subject/occasion	Place
27 May 1879	AT presides at Metropolitan Free Libraries Association meeting	London
18 June 1879	ditto	
23 Oct 1879	'The Zulus and Zululand'	Mechanics' Institute, Nottingham
28 Oct 1879	'The Condition of the Zulu People'	Harborne and Edgbaston Institute, Birmingham

Appendix B
Trollope and the Post Office Library*

It is considerably over forty years since the idea of forming a Post Office Library for the use of the clerical staff took shape. A few officers of the Department, with more or less literary tastes, had been struck with the successful efforts made by the officers of the Foreign Branch of the Circulation Office to establish a departmental book club and association of a literary character, and calling to mind the numerous separate efforts which had been made from time to time in other branches to organise reading associations, these officers met together to consider the practicability of combining these various societies in one general association. The first result was the appointment of a committee of members from each department of the Post Office, and one representative of the Foreign Office Literary Club, for the purpose of arranging the necessary details. A prospectus and code of rules for the management of the association were drawn up, and it was then decided to take the opinion of the whole body of officers of the General Post Office upon the proposed scheme. For this purpose a general meeting was held on the 6th November, 1858, in the Returned Letter Room, at which the late Sir John Tilley, KCB (then Mr Tilley), took the chair. [A report appeared in *The Times*, 25 Nov 1858, p. 10.]

That meeting was a notable one, not only in the history of the Post Office Library, but in the annals of the Department itself, and among those who gathered together for the purpose of forwarding so praiseworthy an object as the establishment of a Post Office library were many whose names have become distinguished both within and outside the Post Office. There were Mr Tilley, who so long and ably held the paramount permanent post in the Department; Mr Scudamore, whose name was long a household word; Mr Anthony Trollope, surveyor in Ireland, and Mr Yates, of the Secretary's Office, both of whom distinguished themselves in letters; Mr George Chetwynd, to whose memory the Post Office Savings Bank and Postal Orders are a lasting tribute; Mr Frederic

* Unsigned article in *St Martin's Le Grand*, xii (1902) 131–40.

Hill, brother of the author of Penny Postage; Mr Hide, the first Receiver and Accountant-General; and there were also Mr West, of the Mail Office, Mr Fyfe, Cashier of the Post Office, Mr Alfred Richardson, of the Money Order Office, Mr Edward Page, an assistant secretary, Mr Angell, Mr G. R. Smith, and a host of others of more or less notability in Departmental circles at that time. The speeches were full of enthusiasm, and if they were lengthy they were by no means tedious or uninteresting. Mr Tilley, notwithstanding his aversion to officers of the Department engaging to literary pursuits, supported the object of the meeting at great length, and forcibly pointed out the great value to be derived from the reading of good books. He alluded to the pleasure of the reading man 'happily placed over his new book, cutting the leaves and looking forward to a thorough evening's enjoyment, and wishing for nothing but your absence'. He also called to mind families where reading was a habit, and thought the pleasantest evenings of one's life were passed in the society of such families, especially if the readers were young ladies pretty as well as intelligent. Mr Frederic Hill followed with a long but most interesting and telling speech on the benefits and pleasure to be derived from reading, and the advantages of an institution such as was proposed, referring to Carlyle when he said that 'The true university in these days is a collection of books'. It would be tedious, and, moreover, space will not permit of it, to dwell upon the whole of the speeches which were made at that memorable meeting, – admirable, able and interesting as each of them was; but there are two which possess the additional interest of having been made by men who afterwards earned a foremost place in literature and which are in themselves so full of interest and humour that no apology need be made for reproducing them here. They are the speeches of Anthony Trollope and Edmund Yates. The former spoke as follows:–

Gentlemen, it is a long time since I have been among you as one of the same department to which you belong, and, therefore, there are few here who know me; but I still hold an appointment in the Post Office – the Irish Branch of it.

I am very sorry that the gentleman who was to have seconded this resolution, and who knows you so much better – Mr Potter – is not here. If he had been here, it would have been better; but I am happy to see you all.

There is very little doubt we shall soon be able to claim the assistance his Royal Highness Prince Albert has offered on certain conditions. Those conditions have already been fulfilled, as no one can doubt who has heard that list which at last became almost wearisome. I thought the titles of all the books printed and published within the last three centuries were going to be read out. That we are obliged to the donors out of the Office there can be no doubt. They have shown that liberality which accords so well with the spirit of the age, and the advance of literature. The good nature, kindness, and liberality of those in the Office must be no less acceptable to their brother officers. I am proud to think there are men among us possessed of such literary taste as is evidenced by the possession of these books. There are books named which are only to be found in rare libraries – books of intrinsic merit, deep research, and great value; and apparently they are not purchased for the occasion, but have been given from the libraries of the gentlemen who possessed them.

I do not know that it is for your benefit that I should give a very long speech, but I should be glad to say something with reference to the profession to which we all belong, and which, I think, will be so materially improved, not only in our own Office, but in others, by such efforts as we are making. We belong to the Civil Service. That service has not always been spoken of in the terms I firmly believe it deserves. It has been spoken of as below those other posts to which the ambition of Englishmen attaches itself; but my belief is that it should offer as fair an object of ambition as any other service, and that the manner in which the duties are generally performed by most of those Departments with which I am acquainted, deserves that the men belonging to it should not be placed in a lower position than those in any other service. I, myself, love the Post Office. I have belonged to it ever since I left school. I work with all my heart, and everyone should do the same; then they will rise with the Department, and the Civil Service will rise to the level of any other profession, whether it be the Church, the Bar, the Army, or the Navy. Such efforts as we are now making will lead to that.

This Reading Room should partake of the nature of a club. I have heard the phrase '*esprit de corps*' mentioned. I think that we may insist on it more. There should be a very strong *esprit de corps*. 'Money Orders' should know 'Circulations', and 'Circulations' should know 'Secretaries'. We should all know each other – all

understand the working of each other's offices – and an interest
in the Service would be better induced by a club than by any other
means. I hope that those in whose hands this matter rests – those
who are able to exercise liberality – will see that this club is made
comfortable. You have all been sitting long on deal benches. I hope
we shall get by degrees something better than deal boards – chairs
with comfortable arms – a well-furnished room. We deserve it. I
trust some liberality will be shown us. It will increase by degrees,
but I hope the time will come when we shall be treated to a
comfortable room and comfortable means of enjoying our reading.
We can't be comfortable on a deal board, and without a good fire
and a nice carpet.

I beg to second the resolution.

Mr Yates gave utterance to these words:–

Gentlemen, our late lamented friend, the temporary committee –
whose demise occurred when you passed this resolution appoint-
ing his successor – in drawing up the programme for this evening's
entertainment, acted in a much wiser manner than could have
been expected from one of his tender years. Like the manager of a
theatrical company, he said to himself, 'I shall have a large audience
to-day', and in order to provide adequate entertainment for them,
he picked his men. Accordingly in the forefront he placed his
tragedians, his 'heavy men'; stern and uncompromising in all
matters of detail, unassailable in statistics, and fully armed at every
point to prove how useful it is to blend amusement with instruction.
To them succeeded his light comedian who is now running round
the corner. I need not say with what modesty he painted the lily
of the purity of our motives, and gilded the refined gold of each
ten guinea subscription. The late committee then saw a lazy hulking
looking fellow in the corner, and hit on the plan of giving him a
resolution to propose, which should carry itself, and the excellency
of which should commend itself, to every person present, while
the natural modesty and timidity of the proposer should have no
effect in annulling it with the audience. Gentlemen, I am that lazy
hulking person, and have that resolution to propose, but so sure
am I of its intrinsic merit, that I shall keep you waiting a moment
before I give it you. As the experienced carver hides in the well of
the dish the most savoury morsel for his own eating – as the most
sticky and most saccharine lollipop is kept to coax the refractory

child to bed – as the funny man keeps his best joke for his exit speech, so do I keep back my *bonne bouche* of a resolution, and intend to tickle and titillate your palates a little longer before I set it before you.

From the first moment the notion of this library was started, I had not the slightest dream of failure. I knew it must be a movement attended with success. I felt that Post Office clerks were ready to relieve themselves of the stigma wrapped up in that miserable threadbare joke, that though men of letters, they were illiterate men. I felt sure you would prove yourselves the real Colchester natives. I am borne out in this by seeing that a good many of you have your beards on, and some of you look as if you had been taken early from your beds, whether you are inclined to shell out, a day or two will prove.

I now pass to the subject of my resolution.

An army without a leader – a boat without a stroke oar – a racer without a jockey – a pen without ink – ham sandwiches without mustard – these are all miserable failures, but are not such failures as a public meeting without a kind, gentlemanly, honest, able, impartial chairman. Fortunately we have been able to boast a leader possessed of all these qualifications. Mr Tilley was the fittest person we could have had to take the chair, not only from the long period he has been engaged in the service of the department, and the high position he has always held, but in consequence of his intimate connection with literature, and his relationship to a lady whose name is known throughout the length and breadth of the kingdom, and whose son is as great an ornament to the literary profession as he is to that department to which we all belong.

And now my task is simply to whisper, in the lowest voice possible, that the thanks of this meeting be presented to Mr Tilley, for his kindness in consenting to be our chairman.

As may be imagined from the idea given of the length of the speeches the meeting was a protracted one, and although it commenced as early as 2 o'clock in the afternoon it was far into the evening before it was over. Nevertheless, there was the satisfaction that it was fraught with the utmost success, and the day was, in the closing words of the chairman, Mr Tilley, 'One of the most satisfactory days we have ever passed in connection with the Post Office'.

The outcome of the meeting was, of course, the appointment of a committee of management, and it may be of interest at this distance of time to give the names of the members of that committee. They were: Chairman, Mr F. I. Scudamore; vice-chairman, Mr J. West; Messrs Angell, Baker, Chenery, Chetwynd, Farmer, Hart, Howard, Lovett, Potts, Rablah, Scudamore, Tod, Walshe, West, and Yates. The auditors were Messrs Milliken, G. C. Barlow, and Walliker. The hon. secretary was Mr Chetwynd, and the hon. librarian was Mr Herbert Joyce, while the sub-librarian was Mr A. Key. Such was the constitution of the first committee of our Post Office Library, mostly all being well-known Post Office names, and of whom, so far as the writer knows, not one remains to tell the tale of the early struggle for existence of the now well-founded institution.

Briefly put, the objects of the 'Post Office Library and Literary Association' – to give its full designation – were to comprehend, for the use of such clerks or higher officers of the Post Office as may become members, a permanent library for reference and circulation, news and general reading room, together with a room for occasional lectures, conversations, general meetings, &c. The subscription was to be annual, at the rate of 12s., which entitled a member to one volume from Mudie's Library in addition to the general advantages of the Association, while for every extra 9s. per annum subscribed an additional volume could be had from Mudie's. Life members were also admitted to the advantages enjoyed by ordinary members on the payment of £5, or on presentation of books or other property of the value of £8. Every member received a copy of the rules and regulations, and a card, which was not transferable.

With these objects in view the committee lost no time in proceeding to work, and, such was the progress they made, that by the 2nd of December, 1858, they were able to announce that £215 had been received and promised, and £130 in life subscriptions. The number of annual subscribers enrolled up to that date was 367, while more than 2000 volumes of books had been received. Moreover, the Postmaster-General had granted the Association the use of two rooms in the General Post Office. This was undoubtedly a good start, and on the 3rd January, 1859, the institution was fairly established, when the library and reading room were opened to the members, the rooms assigned being Nos 66 and 67 in the GPO East. It may well be said that the committee had not let the grass grow under their feet, and there is no doubt that this satisfactory result was due in a great measure to the activity and energy of their hon. secretary, Mr George Chetwynd, whose hand may be freely traced in the earliest documents of the Association. Hard worker as Mr Chetwynd undoubtedly was, one marvels how he found time to give so much attention to the initiation and subsequent carrying-on of the Post Office Library, so fully occupied as he then was in a prominent position in the Money Order Office, and at a time when the inception of so vast a scheme as the Post Office Savings Banks must have been busily engaging his mind. Yet there is no question that, for the benefits and advantages which Post Office officials have so long derived from its Library, much is due to Mr Chetwynd's indefatigable labours and untiring zeal.

The formation of the Library has been achieved by donations of money received from various persons, by any excesses of assets over liabilities, and by the presentation of books by persons who have taken a kindly interest in the Association. It may be of interest to briefly look at the names of some of the earliest donors. The late Prince Consort was one of the first to take a warm interest in the Association, and promised assistance should the project to a certain extent be successfully carried out. The late Duke of Argyll – who for so long was Postmaster-General – sent £5 and a letter expressing warm interest. Professor Ansted presented several of his own valuable works; Mr H. G. Bohn, £10 worth of books. Charles Dickens sent *Household Words* in 17 volumes. This was the first donation received, and was sent merely at the suggestion of his friend Edmund Yates, with that readiness which distinguished Mr Dickens, who was always foremost in any good work. Miss Martineau forwarded a donation of several works, such as her *Deerbrook, British Rule in India*, and *History of the Thirty Years' Peace*, ...

One of the largest donations came from Messrs W. H. Smith & Son, of the Strand. They sent two chests of books, containing upwards of 300 volumes, including many of the best works then just published. As Mr Scudamore said, the civility of Messrs Smith was beyond description. They sent their manager to express their warm sympathy in the movement. 'The Post Office', they said, 'does so much for us, and does it so well, that we feel it a privilege to take part in this undertaking', a meed of praise that is very refreshing in these days when there are so many ready to grumble at Post Office methods. Amongst the many who were willing and anxious to support the movement may be mentioned Dr Farr, Lord Goderich, Mr S. C. Hall, the Dean of Westminster, Cardinal Wiseman, Lord Brougham, Dr Jelf, and many others, too numerous to be named here. Within the Department itself the support was most hearty and wide-reaching, officers contributing donations of money or gifts of books. The newspapers, too, gave much help. The proprietors of the *Times* placed a copy of their journal daily at the disposal of the Association for the reading room, and the *Daily Telegraph* and *Insurance Gazette* followed suit, while the proprietors of the *Illustrated London News*, the *Illustrated Times*, the *Athenaeum*, the *Builder*, and the *Literary Gazette* gave much valuable assistance. The public, as a whole, indeed, showed so much sympathy with the Post Office Library and Literary Association that they not only did much to support the permanent library, but they also established the reading room, which is a very attractive feature of the Association.

In the early years of the Association the literary element was a reality, and not only a name, as now, and during the winter months a regular course of lectures was given. . . .

The success which attended the establishment of the Post Office Library has been well maintained during all the years it has now been in existence, and is now part and parcel of official life, at headquarters at all events. Its progress during these years has been sure, though free from any eventful incidents calling for note here. At the present time the permanent library contains over 4000 volumes, many of which are works of fiction, and it possesses a large number of standard works, some of which, such as Ruskin's, have been presented by the authors. The reading room, which is now in the GPO North, is furnished with most of the daily and weekly newspapers, and many of the monthly journals, as well as the latest edition of the *Encyclopaedia Britannica*. It is open to ladies and gentlemen from 9.45 a.m. to 7 p.m. on ordinary week days and until 2 p.m. on Saturdays, and is much taken advantage of by those who wish to make reference or desire a quiet quarter of an hour's perusal of the papers. How the Association is now governed is somewhat of a mystery, as no committee has been elected for many years past, though the regulations provide for the annual election of members of the committee; nor can the year of the last annual general meeting be fixed so long is it since the last meeting was held. That there is a sub-librarian there is no doubt, for he is in daily evidence; but whether or not there is an hon. secretary is open to question, for one sees or hears nothing of him. Nevertheless, the Library continues to be, as it so long has been, a standing and useful institution, and is a source of pleasure and instruction to thousands of omnivorous readers. Its arrangements are carried out in the most satisfactory manner, and never a hitch occurs. That there must be a *Deus ex machina* lurking somewhere in the background can therefore hardly be doubted.

Appendix C
Some Contemporary Reviews of Trollope's Fiction and *'Autobiography'*, and Selected General Appreciations

'Mr Trollope's Novels', *National Review*, vii (Oct 1858) 416–35 [by R. H. Hutton?].

The Times, 23 May 1859, p. 12 [by E. S. Dallas].

Unsigned essay 'Orley Farm', *National Review*, xvi (Jan 1863) 27–40.

'Mr Trollope's Novels', *North British Review*, n.s. i (May 1864) 369–401 [by A. S. Kinnear].

'Mr Anthony Trollope's Novels', *Fortnightly Review*, n.s. v (1 Feb 1869) 188–98 [by J. Herbert Stack].

'Trollope's Irish Novels', *Dublin Review*, lxv (Oct 1869) 361–7.

'The Novels of Mr Anthony Trollope', *Dublin Review*, n.s. xix (Oct 1872) 393–430; 3rd ser. ix (Apr 1883) 314–34.

'Mr Anthony Trollope's Novels', *Edinburgh Review*, clxvi (Oct 1877) 455–8 [by Alexander Innes Shand].

'A Novelist of the Day', *Time*, i (Aug 1879) 626–32 [by T. H. S. Escott].

Obituary, *The Times*, 7 Dec 1882, p. 9 [by Mrs Humphry Ward].

'Anthony Trollope', *Saturday Review*, liv (9 Dec 1882) 755–6; lvi (20 Oct 1883) 505–6.

'From Miss Austen to Mr Trollope', *Spectator*, lv (9, 16 Dec 1882) 1573–4, 1609–11 [by R. H. Hutton].

'Some Recollections of Mr Anthony Trollope', *Graphic*, xxvi (23 Dec 1882) 707 [by Cuthbert Bede].

'Anthony Trollope', *Macmillan's Magazine*, xlvii (Jan 1883) 236–40 [by E. A. Freeman].

'Anthony Trollope', *Nation*, xxxvi, no. 914 (4 Jan 1883) 10 [by Viscount Bryce].

'Anthony Trollope', *Blackwood's Magazine*, cxxxiii (Feb 1883) 316–20 [by Cecilia Meetkerke].

'The Novels of Anthony Trollope', *Dublin Review*, ix (Apr 1883) 314–34.

'Anthony Trollope', *Harper's New Monthly Magazine*, lxvi (May 1883) 907–12 [by Walter Herries Pollock].

'Anthony Trollope', *Century Magazine*, n.s. iv (July 1883) 385–95 [by Henry James]; repr. in *Partial Portraits* (1888).

'An Autobiography', *Athenaeum*, no. 2920 (13 Oct 1883) 457–9.

'An Autobiography', *The Times*, 13 Oct 1883, p. 10; 14 Nov 1883, p. 8 [by A. I. Shand].

'The Boyhood of Anthony Trollope', *Spectator*, LVI (20 Oct 1883) 1343–4 [by Meredith Townsend].

'Mr. Trollope as Critic', *Spectator*, LVI (27 Oct 1883) 1373–4 [by R. H. Hutton].

'An Autobiography', *Academy*, XXIV (27 Oct 1883) 273–4 [by R. F. Littledale].

'Anthony Trollope', *Macmillan's Magazine*, XLIX (Nov 1883) 47–56 [by John Morley and Mrs Humphry Ward].

'Autobiography of Anthony Trollope', *Blackwood's Magazine*, CXXXIV (Nov 1883) 577–96 [by W. Lucas Collins].

'Anthony Trollope', *Good Words*, XXIV (1883) 142–4 [by Mrs Oliphant].

'Last Reminiscences of Anthony Trollope', *Temple Bar*, LXX (Jan 1884) 130–4 [by Cecilia Meetkerke].

'The Literary Life of Anthony Trollope', *Edinburgh Review*, CLIX (Jan 1884) 186–212 [by Alexander Innes Shand].

'Success in Fiction', *Forum*, VII (May 1889) 314–22 [by Mrs Oliphant].

'Anthony Trollope's Place in Literature', *Forum*, XIX (May 1895) 324–37 [by Frederic Harrison].

'Anthony Trollope', *Cornhill Magazine*, X (Mar 1901) 349–55 [by G. S. Street].

See also David Skilton, *Anthony Trollope and his Contemporaries* (1972); J. Olmsted, J. Welch, *The Reputation of Trollope: An Annotated Bibliography 1925–1975* (1978); and N. John Hall, 'Seeing Trollope's *An Autobiography* through the Press: The Correspondence of William Blackwood and Henry Merivale Trollope', *Princeton University Library Chronicle*, XLVII, no. 2 (1986) 189–223.

Index of Names

Index of Places